Moses and Multiculturalism

FLASHPOINTS

The series solicits books that consider literature beyond strictly national and disciplinary frameworks, distinguished both by their historical grounding and their theoretical and conceptual strength. We seek studies that engage theory without losing touch with history, and work historically without falling into uncritical positivism. FlashPoints will aim for a broad audience within the humanities and the social sciences concerned with moments of cultural emergence and transformation. In a Benjaminian mode, FlashPoints is interested in how literature contributes to forming new constellations of culture and history, and in how such formations function critically and politically in the present. Available online at http://repositories .cdlib.org/ucpress

SERIES EDITORS

Judith Butler, Edward Dimendberg, Catherine Gallagher, Susan Gillman
Richard Terdiman, Chair

1. *On Pain of Speech: Fantasies of the First Order and the Literary Rant,*
   by Dina Al-Kassim

2. *Moses and Multiculturalism,* by Barbara Johnson

Moses and Multiculturalism

Barbara Johnson

Foreword by Barbara Rietveld

UNIVERSITY OF CALIFORNIA PRESS

Berkeley   Los Angeles   London

University of California Press, one of the most distinguished
university presses in the United States, enriches lives around
the world by advancing scholarship in the humanities, social
sciences, and natural sciences. Its activities are supported by
the UC Press Foundation and by philanthropic contributions
from individuals and institutions. For more information, visit
www.ucpress.edu.

University of California Press
Berkeley and Los Angeles, California

University of California Press, Ltd.
London, England

Library of Congress Cataloging-in-Publication Data

Johnson, Barbara, 1947–2009.
    Moses and multiculturalism / Barbara Johnson ; foreword by
Barbara Rietveld.
        p.   cm.—(Flashpoints, 2)
    Includes bibliographical references and index.
    ISBN 978-0-520-26254-6 (pbk. : alk. paper)
    1. Moses (Biblical leader).   2. Multiculturalism.   I. Title.

BS580.M6J64   2010
222'.1092—dc22   2009019422

Manufactured in the United States of America

19   18   17   16   15   14   13   12   11   10
10   9   8   7   6   5   4   3   2   1

The paper used in this publication meets the minimum
requirements of ANSI/NISO Z39.48–1992 (R 1997)
(*Permanence of Paper*).

To Shoshana Felman

CONTENTS

FOREWORD

If the story of Moses didn't exist, Barbara Johnson might have invented it to illustrate concepts she began writing about in 1980. "The problem of difference," she wrote in the Opening Remarks to her first book, *The Critical Difference*, "can be seen both as an uncertainty over separability and as a drifting apart within identity." The focus in this new volume functions as a prism through which she looks at the "separability" of the cultures that have contributed to the formation of the Moses figure through stories told by different peoples and how the "drifting apart within identity" played out in each culture that claimed him as its own.

The point of departure in *Moses and Multiculturalism* is the mixed identity that Moses carried within him: he was born a Hebrew, raised as an Egyptian, and married as a Midianite, then returned to Egypt to liberate the slaves from whom he had been estranged. Johnson explores those dimensions through her analyses of the biblical Moses, the Egyptian Moses, the Frances E. W. Harper Moses, Freud's Moses, and others.

"What literature often seems to tell us," Johnson has observed, "is the consequences of the way in which what is not known is not seen as unknown. It is not, in the final analysis, what you don't know that can or cannot hurt you. It is what you don't *know* you don't know that spins out and entangles 'that perpetual error we call life'" (p. xii). In each version of the Moses story, it is the parts of the story that were unknown or unrecognized that give away each "difference." Flavius Josephus doesn't depict the idolatry in the Golden Calf episode, Zora Neale Hurston seems to have no inkling that Moses might not be Christian, Thomas Mann makes Moses' mother an Egyptian princess, and so on. Who is the real Moses, and what do these different identities signify?

Multiculturalism may be one of these things we don't know that we don't know; this at least is one of the most fertile and disturbing suggestions of Johnson's most recent study of the idea of difference, identity, and the unknown as it manifests itself in the multicultural icon of Moses. What do we think we know? We know, for example, that the term *multicultural* emerged in the 1960s in Anglophone countries in relation to the cultural needs of non-European migrants. Since that time, it has become such an integral part of our discourse that it has almost lost its meaning. If you Google *multiculturalism,* there are 3,750,000 entries—books, courses, articles, panels, diversity training videos, the Ayn Rand Center for Individual Rights—the list is endless.

Multiculturalism, which has been taken to mean a smorgasbord of cultural identities, is here confronted not only with the difference between identities but also with the difference within identities. Using multiculturalism to explain and explore difference refers to an objective Johnson set forth in *A World of Difference* (1987): "to transfer the analysis of difference out of the realm of linguistic universality or deconstructive allegory and into contexts in which difference is very much at issue in the 'real world'" (p. 2).

In the "real world," this is a good time to look back at a biblical figure who has been analyzed by theologians, historians, biblical scholars, psychoanalysts, and literary critics but rarely as "someone who functions well in a world to which he, unbeknownst to the casual observer, does not belong." This description applies to the millions of immigrants and displaced people who currently find themselves in foreign environments, to people alienated in their own country or their own skin, and to everyone who doesn't "fit."

The idea of functioning well or otherwise in a place to which one—one person, one word, or one concept—does not belong has been a part of my conversations with Barbara Johnson for the past forty years. This study is one more piece in her work that sheds new light, one more story that we have read so often and thought we knew.

Barbara Rietveld

Introduction

Ever since Sigmund Freud published his epoch-making *Moses and Monotheism* at the height of the Nazi Holocaust, the impression of Moses' mono-ness and his role as founder of the Jewish faith has been reinforced. But this book begins with the perception that the story of Moses is at once the most nationalist and the most multiculturalist of all foundation narratives. This does not simply mean that many different nations and liberation movements have adopted the story as their own, although the outlines of the story do seem to have compelling and enduring narrative shape. John Hope Franklin could thus call his classic study of Afro-American history *From Slavery to Freedom* (first published in 1947) and set the pitch to which most subsequent histories would be tuned.[1] Jews every year reenact the story of liberation from Egypt at Passover, and Moses as original lawgiver and divine intercessor forms the heart of the Jewish tradition. And when Dante, in one of the basic texts of the European canon, wants to explain allegory in his letter to Con Grande, he uses the story of Moses as a paradigmatic example:

> "When Israel went out of Egypt, the house of Jacob from a barbarous people, Judea was made his sanctuary, Israel his dominion." Now if we look at the letter alone, what is signified to us is the departure of the

sons of Israel from Egypt during the time of Moses; if at the allegory, what is signified to us is our redemption through Christ; if at the moral sense, what is signified to us is the conversion of the soul from the sorrow and misery of sin to the state of grace; if at the anagogical, what is signified to us is the departure of the sanctified soul from bondage to the corruption of this world into the freedom of eternal glory. And although these mystical senses are called by various names, they may all be called allegorical.[2]

Thus, by doing a certain figurative reading of the story of Moses, Dante produces both allegory and Christianity. Starting out from the "new" testament, the Bible becomes "old," and the "old testament," a reservoir of typologies and foreshadowing of the story of Christ.

But already in the Bible, the story of Moses is a multicultural story, a passing narrative, the story of someone who functions well in a world to which he, unbeknownst to the casual observer, does not belong. All the time he is in the Egyptian palace, Moses performs military exploits and has such a noble character that Pharaoh treats him as he wishes to treat his own flesh and blood, which indicates that for Pharaoh, at least, he is not. Whether Moses is cognizant of his own birth and identity is less clear: the Bible is not explicit about it, and later versions have to decide when, and with what consequences, Moses finds out. According to the biblical story, though, there is little doubt that from an outside view Moses was born a Hebrew, raised as an Egyptian, and married as a Midianite and only then goes back to Egypt to liberate the slaves. While he therefore seems to be liberating "his" people from bondage, why does the Bible make such a point of estranging him from them? Why do they so often grumble against him?

The beautiful bass voices that have sung "Go Down, Moses" have not entirely obscured the ambiguity of who is saying what to whom. It is not Moses who tells old Pharaoh to "let my people go" but rather God. Moses is thus God's spokesman, and the people he leads out of slavery are God's people. But the well-known refrain that shouts out "Let my people go!" cannot really represent quotation marks: one of the cruxes in the biblical story and others is thus the extent to which Moses transmits God's message or his own, and who "my" people refers to. When Zora Neale Hurston titles a chapter of her autobiography "My People," she alludes to the affectionate rejection of members of a group to which one belongs. This is one expression that brings up the question of Afro-American ethnicity, along with the story of freeing the slaves, which, as we have seen, fits the story of American slavery almost too well. There are always some family members who reveal *precisely* those traits one has learned to squelch. If "my people" manifests what I least want observers to think I am (and very likely their ready stereotypes, which I have worked so hard to combat), what are *God's* people? Is there some fundamental ambivalence in the claim of possession for God, too? Are his "chosen people" a block to the possibility of idealization?

During Seder dinners, participants repeat the story of Moses and generalize God's goodness in the freeing of all unfree peoples. Haggadot differ in how explicit they are about Auschwitz or Darfur. But all of them function as both a commemoration and a lesson, complete with questions for the uninitiated and explanations of what is being celebrated. The story is often told as if it *happens* to the addressee. The following are examples from two different Haggadot:

> Remember the day on which you went forth from Egypt, from the house of bondage, and how God freed you with a mighty hand. (Union Haggadah, Central Council of American Rabbis, 1982)

> Let us raise our cups in gratitude to God that this call can still be heard in the land. Let us give thanks that the love of freedom still burns in the heart of our fellowmen. Let us pray that the time be not distant when all the world will be liberated from cruelty, tyranny, oppression and war. (Reconstructionist Haggadah, 1942)

The service ends with the Zionists' hope, "Next year in Jerusalem," which can be literal or figurative. The Passover ritual, which announces itself as a repetition, is thus often a commentary on current events. Far from being the same every time, its point inheres in what it talks about, not in what it says.

But nevertheless, its forms of address are designed to call and inform the Jews about their historical position. Moses is merely the means of bringing about Divine history. The relationship celebrated at Passover is between God and Israel.

In both the Koran and the Torah, God is often directly quoted. In the Bible, he is often speaking to Moses. Many chapters of the Book of Exodus begin, "Then the Lord said unto Moses." In the Koran,[3] God often speaks to the believer directly, saying either "We" or "I." The Koran and some Jewish prayers insert "Praised be he" or "praise be unto him" when mentioning someone whose Word is God's. The mysterious name of God—"I am who am"—in the Bible is also a way to turn the third person into a first person. The Omnipotent Subject cannot be an object of speech.

The Koran makes a point of celebrating God, not Moses, or even Mohammed. It takes very seriously its monotheistic strictures and condemns as polytheistic Christianity for divinizing Christ. Its name for the other of Islam is "idolatry." It explains that God the creator has only to say "be," and something is brought into being, whereas idols are not makers but *made* things. God creates by willing; he does not beget: unlike his creatures he has no need for sexual reproduction. God is that to which man should worshipfully submit. An "idol" is not just a forbidden "graven image" but a hated version of the polytheism that is being left behind. Unquestioning faith earns one a pleasant afterlife, while unbelievers will burn in hell. Moses, Mohammed, and Jesus are alike in being mere prophets, to whom God reveals his Scriptures, the Torah, the Gospel, and the Koran. They coexist and complement each other, and the Koran repeatedly mentions with respect the lineage it wants to emphasize: Abraham, Ishmael, Isaac, Noah, Lot, Jacob, Jonah, Moses, Jesus, David, and Solomon. The emphasis on Noah is interesting: not only does it show God's impulse to destroy his creation, but the saving ark he tells Noah to build is the only other place in the Bible where the word for baby Moses' aquatic vehicle of escape is used. God shows his holiness through "signs" like the magic of the staff turning into a serpent or the parting of the sea. The Koran emphasizes the opposition between Moses and Pharaoh, but not Moses as the lawgiver, and equates with divinity the magic that Judaism is embarrassed by. For Islam, then, what is rejected is "form," and the observance of the second commandment is tantamount to avoiding idolatry per se. Koranic "monotheism" is anti-idolatry, like Judaism, but not anti-magic, and it is even more strict than Judaism in equating sin with form. Writing and Revelation are a communication from God, not man, and God shows repeatedly the Paradise reserved for believers, and the eternal Fire that awaits the evildoers on the Day of Judgment. Islam is like Christianity in its belief in the afterlife and the resurrection of the body; it is like Judaism in its respect for laws.

For all Islam's respect for "the book," however, it repeatedly refers to the Koran as "recited," and thus the vehicle of God's truth is a voice, not a scripture. Therefore, it is very fitting that the story of Moses, as told in the Koran, begins with God's voice speaking out of the burning bush. When Moses tries to go around the bush in order to detect why it burns without being consumed, God stops him and tells him to take off his shoes in awe. What sets Moses on his mission is a voice.

The bush that burns without being consumed reminds me of the most memorable use of a terminal adverb in the English language. In Shakespeare's Sonnet 73, there are three metaphors for approaching death: autumn, evening, and a dying fire. The end of the sight of almost-extinguished embers is "consumed with that which it was nourished by." But precisely, this fire is neither nourished nor consumed. God tells Moses that he is no longer in the domain of scientific explanation and mortality but in the domain of the holy, the eternal.

As one might expect, by far the largest number of books that attempt to retell the story of Moses are in the Jewish tradition, and unabashedly rely exclusively on the Bible. Their effort is not at all to showcase the tale's multiplicity but to transmit pedagogically the "real meaning" of the first five books of the Bible (the Books of Moses)—to make sense of Judaism itself (no small task!).

A book by the great authority in matters religious and philosophical, Martin Buber, is called *Moses: The Revelation and the Covenant,*[4] a title that indicates where the author's emphasis lies. On the one hand, he tries to get at what can be learned about God; on the other, what is expected of God's "chosen people." The story of Balaam told in Numbers gives a good picture of the kind of soothsayer Moses was *not*. Yahweh was a new kind of god, and Moses was a new kind of messenger, neither priest nor prophet. The person of Moses has much less interest for Buber than the nature of God's relation to Israel. His preoccupation with *that* leads him to explore seminomadic tribal behavior and the exact function of a portable holy Tabernacle, which can become fixed if the tribe reaches its destination (and is destroyed when that place is destroyed). Although he is not in search of a "historical Moses," he does often call something "the oldest layer" and uses his knowledge of Hebrew, literary forms, and the rest of the Bible to make his points. The book consists of many little chapters that zoom in on subsidiary details, to which he brings immense and sometimes sententious erudition: "And at an unknown hour they pass out of our ken. The Word alone endures" (140). Impatient with biblical scholarship ("It may be enough to mention at this point that I regard the prevailing view of the Biblical text, namely as largely composed of 'source materials' ['Yahwist', 'Elohist', etc.] as incorrect" [8]), he dispenses unargued intuitions from the height of his authority, so that his *Moses* reads like a series of random thoughts from a master teacher.

Michael Walzer's *Exodus and Revolution* studies the ways in which the Moses story has functioned as an inspiration for social change all over the world.[5] But his main politico-religious analysis is reserved for the way in which the Bible cools the optimism of the initial liberation and depicts the inevitable "backsliding," "chiding," and "murmuring" of a people liberated from external—but not internal—oppression. His analysis of internalized second-class citizenship (the longing to return to "the fleshpots of Egypt") plus his remarks about the renewal of the Covenant turn his "revolution" into a much tamer kind of social contract, the father's murder into an agreement among brothers. The paternal principle is no longer the defeated Pharaoh or Old Regime but the Lord of the fathers of Israel who continues to guide and promise. In other words, the theory of government in Exodus is not at all opposed to there being a father, as long as he is both omnipotent and infallible. Moses, too, has to learn to submit to the might of this jealous god, but Moses does not become a founding "father." He has a role to play as God's intermediary, but the people worship the God of Gods. Walzer ends up theorizing a very active "consent of the governed"—really a "participation of the governed." His summary of Exodus politics runs as follows:

> First, that wherever you live, it is probably Egypt;
> Second, that there is a better place, a world more attractive, a promised land;
> And third, that "the way to the land is through the wilderness."[6]
> There is no way to get from here to there except by joining together and marching.[7]

The best-selling American novel by Leon Uris, *Exodus*,[8] makes use of the melodramatic aspects already in the story. Against a backdrop of human pettiness versus a great cause, he foregrounds human complexity and heroism, using just enough characters to tell the outlines of history through individuals. He sets up and counts on erotic tensions that declare themselves in the end while making his novel a tragedy in which every character ends up suffering a great loss. There are many delays in the Scriptures that can easily be transformed into suspense, and he knows how to use suspense: the ten plagues, the Ten Commandments, the murmurings in the wilderness, the night of the Passover when the children of Israel waited to leave with their shoes on, the impatience of the people when Moses tarried on the mountain, which led them to make a golden calf. . . . At the same time, there is no doubt as to where his sympathies lie. The Arabs surrounding Israel are often depicted as greedy, lazy, and cowardly: "The leader of the dreaded El Husseinis was the most vile, underhanded schemer in a part of the world known for vile, underhanded schemers" (253). Arabs, "with murder, rape, and plunder in their hearts" (466), "wantonly violated every concept of honor" (516). When the novel was first published in 1958, the founding of the state of Israel was still a miracle, and memories of the Holocaust were fresh. Gas chambers, concentration camps, the Final Solution—one didn't need to make up the drama inherent in the history of the Jews. The idealism of the early settlers was untarnished; the unending persecution of the Jews goaded them into superhuman action; the whole drama of Israeli independence seemed like a replay of the story of David and Goliath. According to Uris, the sleazy

Arab nations surrounding Israel could have easily integrated the Palestinian refugees, but they chose to keep them in easily inflammable refugee camps they could use for political purposes. The Jewish settlers had redeemed land the Arabs hadn't wanted for centuries, made it productive, and in the process raised the living standards of both Jews and Arabs.

As for the remains of Western Imperialism, it is the Jews, not the Arabs, who suffer from it, and not from the Zionists but from the British. While dividing up the "free" world, the Western powers saw a danger in Jews overrunning Palestine after World War II, and the British, who at that time controlled Palestine, set up detention camps in Western Europe and ringed Palestine with a blockade. Our entry into the novel takes place in the detention camps in Cypress, focalized by two non-Jewish Americans, Mark Parker, who soon drops out of the book, and Kitty Fremont, who wants to go back to America but is always impelled to stay because of her attachment to two Jews, one a substitute for her dead daughter and the other (unavowed) a gigantic and enigmatic but indefatigable freedom fighter. We enter the story on the eve of an illegal departure by the aptly named ship *Exodus,* which is allowed to make the trip thanks to a hunger strike of those on board, as the British replay the refrain of Moses to Pharaoh, "Let my people go" (188). I think this gliding focalization helps the novel grip its American readership. The spectacle of good versus evil is played out for American eyes, and with biblical resonance. Indeed, the map of Israel reads like an Advent calendar in finding a biblical story behind every spot. There is no ambivalence to mar the absoluteness of this fight: this is Israeli politics of 1958, not 2009. Human complexity inheres in individual characters, not world politics.

There have been two notable recent popular/scholarly books about Moses: Jonathan Kirsch's *Moses: A Life* and Joel Cohen's *Moses: A Memoir.*[9] Kirsch collates the considerable body of scholarship that has grown up around the biblical Moses and makes it into an interesting character study. Cohen tries to imagine from the inside what it felt like to be Moses; again the basic source is the Bible, and the goal, the coherence of a person's inner life. And finally, *Exploring Exodus* by Nahum Sarna is the only text about Moses that devotes as much attention as the original text to the Tabernacle (complete with drawings).[10]

The aim of coherent unity, which may not even be possible in the biblical version, collapses with the multiple sources I shall read here. In this book, there can be no search for the "real Moses." Anomalous elements will not fit into some larger picture, and each version will have a center of gravity different from the others while still taking off from something actually in the Bible. The texts have in common only the prestige of the story they are part of, and perhaps a desire to liberate it to make sense in a new way.

Every rewriting of the Moses story has, among other things, to interpret the expression "chosen people." Freud, for example, sees the "chosen people" as a trigger for sibling rivalry. But perhaps until "blood" and "choice" are conflated, until their differences are not the basis of democracy, until a truly democratic regime is not grounded in blood and soil, it is not common blood that unites the "chosen people." At first Moses goes about his task with somewhat the same resignation as that depicted by Robert Frost: "Home is the place where, when you have to go there, / They have to take you in."[11] But to form an equally unbreakable bond through arbitrary will—to have not *families we're stuck with* but *families we choose* (as the title of a book on gay families has it)—puts the "chosen people" in a different light. That Moses is a Hebrew may be both a nationalist sop and a false lead; the biblical story is as long as it is because the Hebrews have to learn to treat Moses as *not* one of their own. Perhaps Moses has to have been acculturated precisely in the household of the enemy in order to lead the enslaved Hebrews out of Egypt. In any case, each of the many versions of the Moses story we will read here has something to say about the sense of the two cultures that go into his formation.

The Bible turns out not to be alone in positing foreignness as somehow necessary for nation building. It itself says many times that one must respect the strangers in one's midst: "But the stranger that dwelleth with you shall be unto you as one born among you, and thou shalt love him as thyself; for ye were strangers in the land of Egypt" (Lev. 19:34). The political theorist

Bonnie Honig sums up the recurring importance of foreigners in foundation narratives as follows:

> Sometimes, the figure of the foreigner serves as a device that allows regimes to import from the outside (and then, often, to export back to outside) some specific and much-needed but also potentially dangerous value, talent, perspective, practice, gift, or quality that they cannot provide for themselves (or that they cannot admit they have). This supplement of foreignness gives receiving regimes something different from the novelty, cultural breadth, and depth identified by theorists of immigration and multiculturalism.[12]

One of the recurring revelations in the various versions of the Moses story from Sigmund Freud to the Egyptologist Jan Assmann is the claim that, far from being a Hebrew, Moses is in actuality an Egyptian.[13] Exactly what, then, is foreign, and to what? Is this story about an individual (Moses) or about a historical process (Exodus)? Does the story begin in Egypt or in Goshen? And is there some Oedipal drama of respect or murder being acted out with each retelling?

II.

One of the most surprising threads that tie all dimensions of this project together is the importance and role of Freemasonry within it, the leadership of brothers tied together not by a covenant but by a secret rite. The fraternal order claims descendency from ancient Egypt and maintains the idea of a secret initiation for the Elect. Faced with the diminished entity that the Masonic order has become in the United States, it is hard for us to imagine its prestige and prominence in eighteenth- and nineteenth-century Europe. The fact that Freemasonry might have derived in part from the medieval guilds of masons, who had to move from place to place and be housed each time near their work site in a lodge, emphasizes the literal importance of architecture in the history of Freemasonry, but its figurative meanings were just as important. From the arts of memory to the rebuilding of Solomon's Temple, the Masons always looked forward to many years of their apocalyptic Craft. Yet the so-called wisdom of the Egyptians that underlay those initiation rites, and into which Moses himself had been initiated according to Acts 7:22, can be textually shown to come at least in part from an eighteenth-century French novel, *Sethos,* by Jean Terrasson. Wolfgang Mozart, for instance, even while being a devoted Mason, initiated in 1784 into the Austrian Lodge Beneficence, unknowingly cites Terrasson when, with his fellow Mason and libretticist, Brother Emmanuel Schikaneder, he depicts a Masonic initiation in his opera *The Magic Flute.*

The U.S. founding fathers were very often Freemasons, which is why they put an unfinished pyramid—one of Freemasonry's occult symbols— on the great seal of the United States. When the early black nationalist Martin Delany was invited to speak in 1853 by the St. Cyprian Lodge #13 of Pittsburgh on the topic of the legitimacy of black masonry, his listeners thought he could simply help straighten out the status of their lodge with the Mother Country, but instead they were told about the origins of Freemasonry itself in ancient Egypt, an African culture. Black Freemasonry, even though forced into existence by white racism, had *more* right to claim legitimacy than did white Freemasonry.

Those who came to the "wilderness" of the New World to seek religious freedom often drew inspiration from the Exodus story. This was particularly true of Puritans, who established a "holy commonwealth" in the Massachusetts Bay Colony and tried to combine God's rule with human rule. John Winthrop (whom Cotton Mather called "the American Moses," soon to be Massachusetts's governor) addressed his congregation aboard the *Arbella* just before landing in 1630 by alluding to Moses ("Thus stands the case between God and us, we are entered into covenant with Him for this work")[14] and ends by quoting what Moses said to the people when he saw the promised land he was never to enter:

> And to shut up this discourse with that exhortation of Moses, that
> faithful servant of the Lord, in his last farewell to Israel, Deuteronomy 30
> [not the King James version], "Beloved, there is now set before us life
> and good, death and evil, in that we are commanded this day to love the
> Lord our God, and to love one another, to walk in his ways and to keep

His commandments and His ordinance and His laws, and the articles of our covenant with Him, that we may live and be multiplied, and that the Lord our God may bless us in the land whither we go to possess it."[15]

As the doyen of Puritan studies in early America, Perry Miller, writes, "'God sifted a whole nation to bring choice grain into the wilderness,' said the Puritan historian."[16] But the Exodus story in fact stands behind a wide variety of pronouncements in the New World: Thomas Morton, an anti-Puritan, who was indeed punished by the Puritans for "bacchanalias" and corruption, could still call his book about America *The New English Canaan*.[17] And later Mary Antin called her book about immigration *The Promised Land*.[18]

But nothing about claiming that land was held to be easy. As a preacher put it in New Haven in 1777, "How soon does our faith fail us, and we begin to murmur against Moses and Aaron and wish ourselves back again in Egypt."[19] Yet often the wish was secretly to be delivered *from* history: from divine guidance to Messianism is but a short step, and Canaan begins to look a lot like Eden.

To say one has God on one's side can justify almost anything; it is an eminently American claim to make. As James Dana put it in a sermon of 1779, "the manifest interposition of the Almighty in humbling tyrants for their sakes" is used by all sides to justify what they are doing.[20] In the fight for American independence from Great Britain, it was all too easy to see Pharaoh in the English crown, Moses in the colonies; tyranny versus freedom. Indeed, the American Declaration of Independence owes a great deal to this underlying myth: "A prince, whose character is thus marked by every act which may define a tyrant, is unfit to be the ruler of a free people."[21]

This was all very well for colonists to say, but they were forgetting the existence of an even greater evil in their midst. As Phillis Wheatley, a slave in Boston, put it in a letter to Samson Occam, an Indian minister raising funds for what would turn out to be Dartmouth College:

By the leave of our modern Egyptians I will assert, that the same Principle [Love of Freedom] lives in us. God grant Deliverance in his own Way and Time, and get him honour upon all those whose Avarice impels them to countenance and help forward the Calamities of their fellow Creatures. This I desire not for their Hurt, but to convince them of the strange Absurdity of their Conduct whose Words and Actions are so diametrically opposite. How well the Cry for Liberty, and the reverse Disposition for the exercise of oppressive Power over others agree,—I humbly think it does not require the Penetration of a Philosopher to determine.[22]

The "free" in "Freemason" was a kind of labor not confined within a guild. But the concept of freedom was very much in fashion: in Kant, it was freedom from natural law; in Locke, it was freedom from inherited privilege; and in political self-justification of all sorts, it was freedom from tyranny and oppression. The French word for Freemason, *franc-maçon,* is a direct translation of the English, but rather than refer to liberty, it somehow brings up the Franks, the Germanic tribes that conquered France. It is no accident that the Barbarians who put an end to the Roman Empire should sound similar to what opposed the church of Rome, condemned by the Protestant Reformation as a return to idolatry.

Freemasonry was born at the same time as—and through the same forces as—the Enlightenment. It was the intellectuals' answer to Catholicism, the religion of the unenlightened European masses. Freemasonry was anti-clerical, even unbelieving, and in Catholic countries an alternative to the Church. Like good French revolutionaries, Masons believed in a Supreme Being and brotherly love. It was the Enlightenment idea of equality that provided the language of the Declaration of Independence and has been the bad conscience of institutions of inequality in the United States ever since. Freemasonry enshrined reason in place of God, but it satisfied the craving for the unexplainable by grounding itself in initiation rites and secrets.

At the time of the Revolutionary War, several blacks were initiated as Masons by an English lodge attached to a military regiment, but, after black men initially fought and died for independence from England, soldiers were eventually segregated into separate regiments by color. Rebuffed by the racism of white lodges, African Lodge #1, under the mastership of Prince Hall, applied to the most worshipful master of Brotherly Love Lodge #55,[23]

London, for a charter from the British Mother Lodge and in 1784 became African Lodge #459. England was thus both the opponent of the consent of the governed and the authority to which one turned for it.

Through African Lodge #459, there grew up the Prince Hall Lodges of the United States, the United Supreme Councils Northern Jurisdiction, and the Southern Jurisdiction of the Scottish Rite.[24] Even the name "Prince Hall" has come to mean "black mason." Manumitted by William Hall, his owner, in 1770, the individual named Prince Hall (if he existed) was able to display his "free" status that made him eligible to become a Mason. Never had the "free" in "Freemason" had so much significance.

Although the ideology of Freemasonry was supposed to be color-blind, the realities were quite different. But whereas the claims of freedom were simultaneous with, and contradicted by, slavery, the segregated lodges grew in importance within their segregated communities. The pillars of those communities often belonged to the Brotherhood, and it was Masonic scruples that kept them exemplary. While Frederick Douglass and many others complained that Freemasonry had "swallow[ed] up the best energies of many of our best men, contenting them with the glittering follies of artificial display,"[25] this apparent fondness for fancy dress and elaborate initiations, the signs of an institution of pure prestige, constituted perhaps the price of functioning as responsible members of the community.

Once one has granted that Egyptian culture is African, the door is open for everything else that belongs to African culture to saturate the text. When Zora Neale Hurston rewrites the story of Moses, his ability to converse with animals and his magic powers make him the consummate conjure-man. As Moses' father-in-law, Jethro, writes to an annoying cousin:

> P.S. Yes, my son Moses is the finest hoodoo man in the world and my wife says that stopping you from eating somebody else's groceries is his greatest piece of work. But she may be wrong.
> Have you ever seen his sendings of snakes and lice?[26]

The religiously embarrassing presence in the Bible of God's magic tricks has always called for some explanation. But Hurston revels in them and celebrates Moses' "MIGHTY HAND." And yet even she is not always sure what she wants Moses' identity to be. When he kills the Egyptian overseer, he feels an unprecedented sympathy for the oppressed: it is not because of identification with the downtrodden that he kills their overseer; it is only *after* he performs this murder that he identifies with those who struggle under the lash. At times, Hurston makes him sound like a white liberal:

> The [Hebrew] foreman approached Moses respectfully and shook his head sadly as he explained, "Some of them want to knock off early to hold a protest meeting, and the others agree with me that it just wouldn't do. It would look bad to my over-boss that just as soon as a Hebrew got to be foreman, the men left work whenever they got ready to hold meetings."
> "Your foreman is right," Moses agreed, speaking to the men. "This sort of thing is what I'm working for."[27]

In spite of Hurston's constant mention of the role of linguistic styles, no character can be identified with the consistency of his language.

In each of the retellings of the Moses story, quite different things are emphasized, but even in the biblical version there are imperfectly integrated or unexplained elements that cannot be easily made into a coherent story (When did Moses marry the Ethiopian princess? Why did Zipporah abruptly circumcise his sons?). What I hope to do in this book, then, is to acquaint readers with the truly bizarre aspects of even the versions of the Moses story they know well, and introduce them to some reimaginings they might not be aware of yet.

Because of Freud's title, Moses has been seen as more mono-, more interested in oneness, than he in fact is. It is my hope to be able to account in this book both for the appeal of the mono- and for the ineradicable presence of the diverse in the story that purports to tell the origins of nationalism.

CHAPTER ONE

The Biblical Moses

And when the Lord saw that he turned aside to see, God called
unto him out of the midst of the bush, and said Moses, Moses.
And he said, Here am I.

Exodus 3:4

This chapter is devoted to reading the original story of Moses and noting the many odd things that come up in it. The story stretches over the Books of Exodus, Leviticus, Numbers, and Deuteronomy, but barely a tenth of that length is devoted to familiar plot elements: the baby in the bulrushes, the killing of the overseer, the burning bush, the liberation from Egypt, the parting of the Red Sea, the rock that gives water, the march through the wilderness to reach the Promised Land, the tables of the law, the Golden Calf. Many chapters are not narrative at all but quote God giving to Moses additional laws, instructions about building the holy Tabernacle, and descriptions of what Levite priests should wear. A smaller number narrate episodes such as Korah's rebellion or the encounter with Balak and Balaam. Why do we read the Bible so selectively? What is the function of all God's instructions we tend to leave out? And what about episodes deemed inexplicable?

One of the most puzzling cruxes occurs on the way from Midian to Egypt, where Moses has been commanded by God to lead the Israelites to freedom. One night, God seeks to kill Moses, whereupon Zipporah, Moses'

Midianite wife, who has accompanied him, picks up a sharp rock, cuts off the foreskin of their son (who also accompanies them), throws the cut-off mass at his (whose?) feet, and declares, "a bloody husband art thou to me" (Exod. 4:24–26). God lets Moses go. What does this all mean?

In the Pentateuch edited by J. H. Hertz, this passage is glossed in part as follows:

> *sought to kill him.* An anthropomorphic way of saying that Moses fell suddenly into a serious illness. Many commentators connect this sudden illness of Moses with his postponing, for some reason, the circumcision of his son. Tradition ascribes this omission to the influence of Jethro and Zipporah, who may have desired the circumcision postponed to the 13th year, as was customary among the Bedouin tribes. However, in the previous verse Moses had warned Pharaoh that disobedience of God's will carried dire punishment with it: and he himself should, therefore, on no account have permitted any postponement of a duty incumbent upon him.[1]

Thus, through this literal and empirical reading of the passage, it seems as though all obscurities have been cleared up, at least enough of them for the consequences of failing to do one's duty to come through loud and clear.

The transformation of unclarified questions into useful lessons is even more apparent in the Pentateuch published in 1986 by the Judaica Press, with extracts or summaries of the commentary of Samson Raphael Hirsch.[2] The more enigmatic, the more didactic, it seems.

> 24. *[God confronted him.]* The same God Who had just sent Moses forth with a most lofty mission, which Moses was preparing to carry out, now abruptly confronted him and considered it better that he should die. The verses that follow make it clear why Moses was so suddenly placed in danger of death. He had neglected to circumcise his son. He had gone forth to accomplish the deliverance whose import would be based solely on *milah* [the word—B.J.], and now he himself was about to introduce into that people an uncircumcised son. God considered it better to have Moses die than to have him set out on his mission with such an unfortunate example for his people.
>
> This, it seems to us, should be the interpretation of ["considered it

better . . . "] Interpreted literally as ["and He sought (to kill him)"], it would be a very harsh characterization of God. God the All-Merciful never "seeks" to "kill" a man; if it is His will that a man should die, then that man will die. But interpreted in the manner suggested here, this passage teaches us the significant lesson that the plans of God cannot be influenced by *any* human being. . . . To God no man, not even one such as Moses, is indispensable. . . .

   25. *[Hirsch cites a statement by Rabbi Eliezer of Modai in the Mekhita to Parshath Yithro (Exodus 18:1–20:23) to the effect that Yithro had agreed to have Tzipporah marry Moses only under the condition that the first son of this union should remain a heathen and not be circumcised. Also, Hirsch points out that Tzipporah, not being of Jewish origin, may have been naturally reluctant to see her son undergo the pain and the dangers of circumcision. . . . She therefore quickly circumcised her son with her own hands, cast the boy's foreskin at her husband's feet and said to him, as Hirsch puts it: "I have done this because you have become a 'bridegroom of death' on my account."]*

   26. *[According to Hirsch, Tzipporah felt that this incident would ensure the observance of circumcision for all time to come. If even a man like Moses, who had been charged with a Divine mission, nearly lost his life for failing to circumcise his son, what Jew in future would dare be guilty of the same neglect?]*[3]

Circumcision, then, in Moses' day as well as in ours, is a sign in the flesh of all newborn males of membership among God's "chosen people." It is also a sign of the covenant God established with Abraham and renewed with Moses. In other words, it is the visible sign of belonging; a sign of voluntary submission and sanctification.

   By the time Saint Paul (né Saul) plays around with the flesh and the spirit in order to explain Christianity, the inadequacy of having circumcised flesh without the corresponding circumcised spirit—indeed, the sufficiency of having spiritual faith, whether or not one has a sign of sanctification in the body—the specialness of the body becomes literal, while the spiritual becomes figurative. Judaism, as Paul explains it, is legalistic and literal, but Christian goodness is a spiritual grace that requires no law. If one strictly observes the laws of Judaism, one remains only within the law, but with Christ, one rises above it.

Moses indeed becomes the mouthpiece of a vast array of detailed laws, as we shall see, but he also appears to be the first user of "circumcision" in a figurative sense. Long before the birth of Christ, and simultaneous with the very origins of biblical Israel, in other words, Moses can cry out to God (twice):

> And Moses spake before the Lord, saying, Behold the children of Israel have not hearkened unto me; how then shall Pharaoh hear me, who am of uncircumcised lips? (Exod. 6:12)

> And Moses said before the lord, Behold, I am of uncircumcised lips, and how shall Pharaoh hearken unto me? (Exod. 6:30)

The Judaica Press edition of the Five Books of Moses avoids the difficulty by translating "uncircumcised" lips as "unpliant" lips. The Hertz edition says, "*of uncircumcised lips, i.e.,* with lips closed or impeded, not properly prepared to deliver an all-important message."[4] This constitutes a medical reading of "uncircumcised lips": the surgical sense of genital cutting is transferred upward to Moses' already known difficulties with speech. Nevertheless, Moses shows himself a canny manipulator of the figurative potential of even the most surgical meaning of circumcision. As Jonathan Kirsch puts it, "Even something so basic and so concrete as the ritual of circumcision was put to use by Moses as a metaphor for an even more intimate commandment. 'Circumcise therefore the foreskin of your heart,' thundered Moses, suggesting that God sought a heartfelt spiritual commitment and not merely a sign carved into the flesh (Deut. 10:16)."[5] It did not take Christianity, in other words, to imagine a correspondence between the spirit and the flesh, but it *did* take Christianity to imagine them so far apart.

What *about* Moses' speech difficulties, anyway? Why does Moses, in his third attempt to depict his lack of authority to speak for the Israelites, tell God, "O my Lord, I am not eloquent, neither heretofore, nor since thou hast spoken unto thy servant: but I am slow of speech, and of a slow tongue" (Exod. 4:10). There have been many theories to explain Moses' speech impediment. Especially since this passage is followed by one in which an exasperated God says to Moses, "Is not Aaron the Levite thy brother? I know that he can speak well. . . . And he shall be thy spokesman unto the people: and he shall be, even he shall be to thee instead of a mouth, and thou shalt be to him instead of God" (Exod. 4:14, 16).

One explanation, then, is that Aaron is a more eloquent public speaker than Moses, and will be believed by the suspicious Israelites. Schoenberg, as we will see, built his whole opera, *Moses and Aaron*, around this opposition between Aaron's eloquence and Moses' message.

Here is what Hertz has to say about it:

> *slow of speech, and of a slow tongue.* Lit. 'heavy of speech and heavy of tongue.' He may have had an actual impediment in his speech. Rabbinic legend tells that Moses when a child was one day taken by Pharaoh on his knee. He thereupon grasped Pharaoh's crown and placed it on his head. The astrologers were horror-struck. 'Let two braziers be brought'—they counselled; 'one filled with gold, the other with glowing coals; and set them before him. If he grasps the gold, it will be safer for Pharaoh to put the possible usurper to death.' When the braziers were brought, the hand of Moses was stretching for the gold, but the angel Gabriel guided it to the coals. The child plucked out a burning coal and put it to his lips, and for life remained 'heavy of speech and heavy of tongue.'[6]

The explanation in the Hirsch volume goes as follows: "'I have difficulty starting to speak, under any circumstances; besides, I have a lisp. I have no command over my tongue.' It is sad when a public speaker, particularly one who seeks to sway large audiences, can elicit nothing but laughter from his listeners . . ."[7] And Nahum Sarna glosses Moses' reluctance to answer God's call as follows:

> He who would be a leader of people, a spokesman who has to negotiate Egyptian court, must possess oratorical skills. But Moses feels himself to be inadequate to the task. He lacks persuasive eloquence. Whether the text means that he literally suffers from some speech defect or that after the passage of years away from Egypt his fluency in the language of the land had deteriorated,[8] or whether he simply asserts his inexperience and native reserve regarding the art of public speaking, it is hard to say.[9]

All the commentators I have read, in other words, see in Moses' worries about speaking for the children of Israel some sort of *personal* characteristic—whether a stammer or a native reserve—that makes him ill equipped to perform his task. But what if Moses' "uncircumcised lips" have simply not been sanctified by a lifetime of faithful service to the God of Abraham? What if he has strayed far away from the God of his fathers, as his brother Aaron has not? Moses is quick to collaborate with God in making Aaron chief priest and making the priesthood belong to Aaron's family. Of course, it's Moses' family, too, so Moses' designation of the Levites as priests may have other motives.

But, in any case, it makes sense if the task of leading people much more knowledgeable about things Jewish should give Moses pause. And indeed the people's quickness to doubt him is attested in many subsequent episodes. The Egyptians, as well as the Hebrews, circumcised their male children, and so, somewhere along the way, Moses was no doubt circumcised. But as the sign of participation in God's covenant, Moses was clearly right to see others as more qualified. On the other hand, who was more equipped to speak to Pharaoh? This adds to the ambiguity of the expression "Let my people go" and brings us back to the question of political representation. God's spokesman, with some justice, has major doubts about his ability to perform the role.

The second half of the Book of Exodus and most of Leviticus, Numbers, and Deuteronomy as well are transcriptions of God's words to Moses or Moses' to the people, detailing the laws and ordinances by which the children of Israel are expected to live. The episode of the Golden Calf leads to a detailed description of how to make the Lord's Tabernacle. Many of God's instructions concern the proper procedures for sacrifices, the proper behavior and dress for the priests, and the proper form for worship. It will be recalled that the first request Moses and Aaron make to Pharaoh is to let the Israelites go three days into the desert and sacrifice to their Lord. Whether or not this is a covert request for freedom, it indicates that it is considered perfectly natural to renew the covenant with, and propitiate, one's newly restored god.

As for the detailed instructions for building a movable tabernacle, they must be meant to contrast with that most loathed form of worship, idolatry. The same golden earrings that, melted, go into the making of the form of a calf can be pounded thin to cover the parts of the Tabernacle. The making of a *place* for a god is quite different from making the *form* of a god. And the Tabernacle had to be mobile because the people were mobile. Their god was not visualizable—indeed, not visible—but nevertheless could be a presence among them as they wandered. The land he promised to them was not uninhabited, but he would ensure their victory. He said to his people, not "I am the only god," but "Thou shalt have no other gods before me." In other words, this invisible god who claimed the loyalty of the people wanted an exclusive relation with them, and was different from other gods. He had no form—could not be the basis for an image—and, like the serpent into which Aaron's rod was changed, he ate up all others. This god's monotheism was in fact a victory over polytheism, idolatry, and, later, the Canaanites. Worshiping a golden calf was a double abomination: going back to idolatry and having another god before him. As Moses repeatedly tells the doubting people, "Your murmurings are not against us, but against the Lord" (Exod. 16:8).

With all this emphasis on what made this god different from others, it is not surprising that he would give extensive instructions about how to build the Tabernacle and how to worship. He also supplements the Ten Commandments with many rules dictated to Moses.

The function of writing is also new, and unclear. Moses takes dictation from God about the laws of his covenant, and Moses is called the author (or scribe) of the first five books of the Bible. There was a huge difference between Egyptian writing (hieroglyphics—pictorial—thus, idolatrous) and God's writing (Hebrew—nonpictorial). Moses thus inaugurated the sacred script in which the Bible is written. The prohibition on graven images is a prohibition on images: twice in his instructions about the Tabernacle God refers to engraving—but always of words, not of images. The priest is to wear on his shoulders the names of the tribes of Israel "like the engravings of a signet" and fashion a plate of pure gold that says, "HOLINESS TO THE LORD" (Exod. 28:11, 36). God appears in a cloud and a fire—*signs* of divinity but not at all images. God's finger writes—and Moses rewrites—the two tables containing the Ten Commandments, which Moses, in his anger at the people's "corruption," broke. Two "Tables of Testimony" are supposed to be put in the ark of the Tabernacle, but whether this means, as it seems to in Exodus, the stone tablets containing the Ten Commandments or the Torah that Moses is in the process of writing down, as seems to be the holy object today, is not clear. In either case, what is sacred is *writing*.

If the large majority of space in the Five Books of Moses is non-narrative, then, it should not surprise us that so much attention is given to God's instructions. Even where there are narrative moments, they tend to be enigmatic:

> And Miriam and Aaron spoke against Moses because of the Ethiopian woman whom he had married; for he had married an Ethiopian woman. (Num. 12:1)

> Take Aaron and Eleazar his son and bring them unto mount Hor: And strip Aaron of his garments, and put them upon Eleazar his son; and Aaron shall be gathered unto his people, and shall die there. (Num. 20:25, 26)

Indeed, the death of Moses on Mount Nebo without entering the Promised Land (Deut. 34:7) is irrefutable proof for some that Moses could not be the author of the Five Books of Moses. Who can narrate his own death?

Who is this Ethiopian woman, and why did Aaron and Miriam speak against Moses for her sake? The Bible tells us no more about her. Josephus narrates Moses' exploits as an Egyptian general, in particular against the Ethiopians, one of whose princesses was so impressed by his valor that she insisted on marrying him. Which didn't prevent Moses from accepting Jethro's gift of one of his daughters. Thus either the Ethiopian woman was Zipporah and the Midianites were dark skinned or this passage is the remnant of a story that Josephus, too, attests. In any case, polygamy was not infrequent among the early Hebrews. But was racism? Did Miriam and Aaron taunt Moses because Zipporah was dark skinned? Or did they chide him for going outside the Israelites, for marrying a Midianite or an Ethiopian, not one of their own people? The Books of Moses spend quite a lot of time detailing the bloodlines of the twelve tribes, and Moses certainly messes up that picture. At the same time, the Bible is full of these "unofficial" families.

CHAPTER TWO

Moses and the Law

Moses is often associated with the founding of the rule of law: a U.S. judge who wanted to display the Ten Commandments in his office sparked an intense debate about the separation of church and state. Christians treated the Ten Commandments as their own; it was Christian fundamentalists who laid down their bodies to prevent the removal of what had become by then a granite version of the commandments in the (by then) disbarred judge's office. Zora Neale Hurston, too, refers to "the Moses of the Christian concept" and seems to have no inkling that Moses might not be Christian.[1] And it is no wonder, finally, that both of DeMille's versions of the story are called "The Ten Commandments." And yet the so-called Books of Moses are mostly filled with dietary laws and decorating tips that have no place in Christianity. Is Moses Christian or Jewish? Christians appropriate his laws as if they were a universal moral foundation; Jews, as if the specificity of their religion started with him. As a founding moment in legal theory, Moses is often seen as providing a rationale for the rule of law.

Arthur Jacobson's "The Idolatry of Rules: Writing Law According to Moses, with Reference to Other Jurisprudences" uses Moses' lawgiving to outline the differences between "static" and "dynamic" law.[2] Jacobson studies the unprecedented references to writing in order to show how the Five Books of Moses insist on the collaborative and not fixed nature of law made by

Moses and God. The people see Moses talking with the god in the fire and cloud on the top of the sacred mountain, while they stay fearfully outside the borders of the sacred, lest they die. When Moses tells them what God has said, they reply several times, "All that the Lord hath spoken we will do" (Exod. 19:8). When Moses breaks the tables God has written, he writes them again. But having a fixed text is just the beginning; Jacobson mentions the years of study it takes to get to know the oral law.

Jacobson does not mention a crucial but puzzling scene in the administration of the law. After the battle with Amalek, early in the relations between the children of Israel and Moses, Jethro, Moses' father-in-law, comes into Moses' camp with Zipporah and Gershom and Eliezer, who had apparently gone back to Midian. After seeing his son-in-law attempt to administer the law entirely by himself, Jethro suggests that it would be less exhausting (and more collaborative) if the cases that can be solved by simply applying a law would be administered by people appointed to fulfill that function, leaving only the difficult cases for Moses. Then the Midianites are again on their way. This scene shows some of the advantages of written law: it does not depend on any individual but allows for easy representation, delegation, and substitution.

In the United States, for example, the written law—say, the Constitution— presents several advantages and several drawbacks for lawmakers. By being written, it cannot be changed by individual whim or historical circumstance. It can only be interpreted. The relations between the oral and the written, in order to keep that fixity, must consider that there is no interpretation in the original writing. But that is belied by the search for "original intent." The seeming impersonality of writing, like the omnipotence of God, is an excuse for not having to think.

Between God's words to Moses and Moses' words to the people, Jacobson often identifies interpretation. To God's order to purify and cleanse in preparation for the third day, Moses seems to add, "Come not at your wives" (Exod. 19:15). Indeed, Moses' interpretations often have the allure of a woman. As Jacobson puts it, "'Interpretation' is necessary. It is also tempting.... He ties the content of his interpretations to temptation and impurity—the necessity and danger, as he regards it, of women."[3]

Jacobson uses the difference between Elohim and Yahweh to get at the difference between a finished law and a changing one. A dynamic jurisprudence, like the collaborative writing between Moses and Yahweh, is written three times. A black-letter, Elohistic, law requires only one or two writings. When the people bow down to the law, the law functions like an idol. In order to avoid idolatry, one should not worship the written law but struggle with it. The interaction between the oral and the written, which is present throughout the relations between God and Moses, renders less certain— more ad hoc—the application of the law.

There are thus not one but three ways Moses brings Israel the law: not only in the famous tables scene, but in the scene of delegation with Jethro and in the transcription of God's voice. In each case, the way is prepared for a substitute lawgiver: writing ensures that the law outlive the lawgiver. Moses is the first writer, but in his writings he transcribes God's voice. The origin of the law is the divine voice:

> This day the Lord thy God hath commanded thee to do these statutes and judgments: thou shalt therefore keep and do them with all thy heart, and with all thy soul.
>
> Thou hast avouched the Lord this day to be thy God, and to walk in his ways, and to keep his statutes, and his commandments, and his judgments, and to hearken unto his voice:
>
> And the Lord hath avouched thee this day to be his peculiar people, as he hath promised thee, and that thou shouldest keep his commandments;
>
> And make thee high above all nations which he has made, in praise and in name and in honour; and that thou mayest be an holy people unto the Lord thy God, as he hath spoken. (Deut. 26:16–19)

The law is inextricable from the holiness of the nation—from monotheism. It is through the people's willingness to subordinate their will to God's that they are his "chosen." It is not because he deserves to be worshiped. The opposition is now between laws and images: the episode of the Golden Calf shows the forbidden idolatry of images.

The story of Moses occupies a small portion of Exodus. The rest of Exodus, Leviticus, Numbers, and Deuteronomy consists of God giving instructions to his people through Moses—instructions about celebrations, sacrifices, the Tabernacle, and things likely to happen in a nomadic community (if one ox gores another or falls in a hole, then ...). The Ten Commandments constitute a small percentage of the laws transmitted by Moses. One striking thing about the laws enounced by God is that they prepare for coming generations: to be a people is to think in terms of generations, not individuals. The Promised Land was promised to the *fathers* (in Genesis), the Levites will always be priests, and so on. The law exists so that individuals can die without affecting the overall scheme. The Five Books of Moses are writings designed to create transference onto the lawgiver and to erase him at the same time.

Thus Moses the lawmaker is complicated. He struggles against the very fixity he represents. Maybe that is his lesson: there is no end to the struggle.

CHAPTER THREE

Flavius Josephus

Josephus was a Pharisee priest, a Jewish historian, and a military leader who wrote around the time of the death of Christ. His opposition to Jewish nationalism and his infatuation with the Roman Empire have negatively affected his reputation among Jews, but his accounts of Jewish history are often the only versions that still exist outside of the Bible. It is from him that we learn extensively about Moses' brilliant early career as an Egyptian general, and there is no reason to question that version's authority.

In addition, Josephus offers a firsthand account (in *The Wars of the Jews*) of the fall of Jerusalem. The dream of rebuilding Solomon's Temple, it will be recalled, is one of the projects that inspire the Freemasons (and is it an accident that the enslaved Israelites were primarily masons, workers in brick if not builders of pyramids?).

The official English translation of the works of Josephus, however, first published in 1736, is another story.[1] The reader needs to look at but also past the copious notes by William Whiston, the translator, "Christianizing" the story of Moses, and bringing it in line with his eighteenth-century beliefs. Since Josephus was writing just after the death of Christ, some of the myths that grew up around Christ also undoubtedly affect Josephus's original tales. In addition, Josephus's original Aramaic version has been lost, so all translations are based on the Greek, which may or may not correspond to

Josephus's intentions. Reading a politically dubious historian translated by someone constantly trying to "convert" the text makes this version of the story particularly challenging—and interesting.

The first spillover between the story of Jesus and the story of Moses concerns the king's motivation for killing the children. Pharaoh, warned that the Israelites would be led out of Egypt by one born at that time, orders the deaths of all the male children. Unlike the biblical tale of drastic population control, this is a tale of rivalry like the one recounted in Matthew:

> Now when Jesus was born in Bethlehem of Judaea in the days of Herod the king, behold, there came three wise men from the east to Jerusalem, saying, Where is he that is born King of the Jews? For we have seen his star in the east, and are come to worship him.
>
> When Herod the king heard these things, he was troubled, and all Jerusalem with him. . . .
>
> And he sent them to Bethlehem, and said, Go and search diligently for the young child; and when ye have found him, bring me word again that I may come and worship him also. . . .
>
> And being warned of God in a dream that they should not return to Herod, they departed into their own country another way.
>
> And when they were departed, behold, the angel of the Lord appeared to Joseph in a dream, saying, Arise, and take the young child and his mother, and flee into Egypt, and be thou there until I bring thee word; for Herod will seek the young child to destroy him. . . .
>
> Then Herod, when he saw that he was mocked of the wise men, was exceeding wroth, and sent forth, and slew all the children that were in Bethlehem, and in all the coasts thereof, from two years old and under, according to the time which he had diligently enquired of the wise men. . . .
>
> But when Herod was dead, behold, an angel of the Lord appeareth in a dream to Joseph in Egypt, saying, Arise, and take the young child and his mother, and go into the land of Israel; for they are dead who sought the young child's life. (2:1–3, 8, 12–13, 16, 19–20)

Here is what Pharaoh says in Exodus: "And he said unto his people, Behold, the people of the children of Israel are more and mightier than we" (1:9). Pharaoh orders the killing of newborn males, first attempting to work through midwives but, when that does not work, charging all his people to drown them in the river: "And the woman [Jochebed] conceived, and bore a son and when she saw him that he was a goodly child, she hid him three months. And when she could no longer hide him, she took for him an ark of bulrushes" (2:2–3). And he is rescued by Pharaoh's daughter and nursed by his own mother:

> And the daughter of Pharaoh came to wash herself at the river . . . and when she saw the ark among the flags, she sent her maid to fetch it. And when she had opened it, she saw the child: and, behold, the babe wept. And she had compassion on him, and said, this is one of the Hebrews' children. Then said his sister to Pharaoh's daughter, Shall I go and call to thee a nurse of the Hebrew women, that she may nurse the child for thee? And Pharaoh's daughter said to her, Go. And the maid went and called the child's mother. And Pharaoh's daughter said unto her, Take this child away, and nurse it for me, and I will give thee thy wages. (2:5–9)

Three verses later, the grown-up Moses goes out among "his brethren" and kills the Egyptian overseer.

In Josephus's *Antiquities of the Jews,*[2] the story is much more detailed, psychological, and supernatural:

> Now it happened that the Egyptians grew delicate and lazy . . . and gave themselves up to other pleasures. . . . They also became very ill affected towards the Hebrews, as touched with envy at their prosperity. (Bk. 2, chap. 9, par. 1, p. 66)

> While the affairs of the Hebrews were in this condition [of hard labor], there was this occasion offered itself to the Egyptians, which made them more solicitous for the extinction of our nation. One of those sacred scribes, who are very sagacious in foretelling future events truly, told the king, that about this time there would a child be born to the Israelites, who, if he were reared, would bring the Egyptian dominion low, and would raise the Israelites; that he would excel all men in virtue, and obtain a glory that would be remembered through all ages. Which thing was so feared by the king, that . . . he commanded that they should cast every male child, born to the Israelites, into the river. (Bk. 2, chap. 9, par. 2, p. 66)

A man, whose name was Amram, one of the nobler sort of the Hebrews, was afraid for his whole nation, lest it fail, by the want of young men to be brought up hereafter, and was very uneasy at it, his wife being then with child.... Hereupon he betook himself to prayer to God ... [who] stood by him in his sleep ... [and] put him in mind, that when Abraham had come alone out of Mesopotamia ... he had been made happy.... Know, therefore, that I shall provide for you all in common what is for your good, and particularly for thyself what shall make thee famous; for that child, out of dread of whose nativity the Egyptians have doomed the Israelite children to destruction, shall be this child of thine. (Bk. 2, chap. 9, par. 3, p. 67)

When the vision had informed him of these things, Amram awaked and told it to Jochebed, who was his wife.... The throes of her delivery did not fall with violence. And now they nourished the child at home privately for three months, but after that time, Amram ... determined to intrust the safety and care of the child to God, than to depend on his own concealment of him.... When they had thus determined, they made an ark of bulrushes, after the manner of a cradle, and of a bigness sufficient for an infant to be laid in, without being too straitened. (Bk. 2, chap. 9, par. 4, p. 67)

Thermuthis was the king's daughter. She was now diverting herself by the banks of the river; and seeing a cradle borne along by the current, she sent some that could swim, and bid them bring the cradle to her. When ... she saw the little child, she was greatly in love with it, on account of its largeness and beauty.... Thermuthis bid them bring her a woman that might afford her breast to the child; yet would not the child admit of her breast, but turned away from it, and did the like to many other women. Now Miriam was by when this happened ... and she said, "It is in vain that thou, O queen, callest for these women for the nourishing of the child, who are in no way of kin to it; but still, if thou wilt order one of the Hebrew women to be brought, perhaps it may admit the breast of one of its own nation." Now since she seemed to speak well, Thermuthis bid her procure such a one.... So when she had such authority given her, she came back and brought the mother, who was known to nobody there. And now the child gladly admitted the breast. (Bk. 2, chap. 9, par. 5, p. 68)

And when one time she had carried Moses to her father . . . she said to him, "I have brought up a child who is of a divine form, and of a generous mind; and . . . I thought proper to adopt him for my son and the heir of thy kingdom." . . . [S]o he took him, and hugged him . . . and on his daughter's account, in a pleasant way, put his diadem upon his head; but Moses threw it down to the ground, . . . and trod on it with his feet; which seemed to bring along with it an evil presage concerning the kingdom of Egypt. (Bk. 2, chap. 9, par. 7, p. 68)

Whereupon the same soothsayer, recognizing the child, sought to kill him, while Thermuthis snatched him to safety, and the king was convinced by God to spare his life. Moses is then educated like a member of the royal household, and the entire episode of military prowess against the Ethiopians, which frightens the king, follows. Moses flees to Midian in the Bible because he fears the consequences of killing the Egyptian overseer, but in Josephus, there is no such episode; Moses flees to Midian because the Egyptians fear his strength.

It is interesting to note that the word for Moses' adversary is, in the *Antiquities of the Jews,* "king," not "Pharaoh." Even in the arguments and plagues brought against Egypt, Josephus's text only occasionally uses the word *Pharaoh.* On the one hand, this reduces much of the Egyptianness of the story: the Pharaonic dynasties were an especially Egyptian form of government: who says "Pharaoh" says "Egypt." On the other hand, the word *king* is more generic: after Moses, Israel had many centuries of kingly rule. The "kings" of card games, checkers, and chess help to inscribe monarchical structures as givens. "King" was the name for the ruler of a people ("King of the Jews") under the rubric of the Roman Empire at the time of Christ. Whereas "Pharaoh" has come to mean "bad king"—and the particular oppression the Israelites were liberated from is always a temptation of kingship—to signify "bad king," a king had to be made "Oriental." On the other hand, it is handy to use "Pharaoh" as shorthand for "tyrant," unfair only to the Egyptians. And to situate tyrannous kingdoms in the East, unfair only to Orientals.

Unlike the Bible, which seems to be written by no one, Josephus is not averse to putting his perspective into print. He speaks of "our nation," though it is well before the era of nation building, and says, "As for myself, I have delivered every part of this history as I found it in the sacred books; nor let anyone wonder at the strangeness of the narration" (*Antiquities*, bk. 2, chap. 16, par. 5, p. 77). His explicit mention of being a Jew perhaps frees him not to toe the party line, while by attributing the "strangeness" of his story to Scripture, he takes no responsibility for the supernatural events he transmits. This particular combination of skepticism and faith reminds one of modern Jewish commentators, who are satisfied that there is divine guidance only when they have found a natural explanation for the "miracles" of the parting of the Red Sea (wind and tides), the plagues (long discourse about a red dye in the Nile, sandstorms, hail, and locusts), quail (they are migrating), and manna ("a secretion of a cochineal insect"). Contrary to what one might be tempted to think, it seems, a miracle can be admitted only if there *could* be a natural explanation for it. The proof of a Divine Plan is shown by miracles that might have occurred naturally. In that way, commentators get to have it both ways: God is behind the miracle, but it could have occurred anyway. If you believe only in the laws of nature, there *is* a scientific explanation; if you need evidence of God's intervention, the unlikeliness of all these events attests to it.

In both the New Testament and Josephus's account of the birth of Moses, God acts on people by means of dreams and visions. In Exodus, it is more likely to see God quoted directly. Josephus's text obeys the laws of realism and allegory. Early allegory often used the premise of dreaming. In the Old Testament, things sometimes occur in no real space: both Abraham and Moses respond to God's call in the same way, by saying, "Here I am." Here? Where?

Speaking of allegory, Josephus's style often sounds a lot like *Pilgrim's Progress* (which also occurs in a dream), more contemporary with Josephus's English translator than with his own life. Indeed, the style, with its use of subordinate clauses and explanatory asides, resembles the style of the early English novel, born around the same time as the translator. The thudding biblical compound sentences have far less flexibility and chattiness than

Josephus's compound-complex sentences. Can one imagine a sentence like "the child, out of dread of whose nativity the Egyptians doomed the Israelite children to destruction," in Exodus? And one of the biblical enigmas consists in the fact that Moses' father-in-law is first called Reuel, then Jethro. For some, this is a clear sign of the attempt to join together multiple versions. Josephus simply says, "Now Moses, when he had obtained the favor of Jethro, for that was one of the names of Raguel . . . " (*Antiquities,* bk. 2, chap. 12, par. 1, p. 71). Josephus tends to leave nothing unexplained, and gives the impression of an author thinking. Whether these stylistic features come from Josephus, his translation into Greek, or the translation into English is unclear, but in any case we are not in Exodus any more. With Josephus, we are often in the realm of the metalinguistic. In the Bible, we are often hearing the primary word.

In Josephus's writing, the greatness of Moses is what is emphasized; in the Bible, God's. Josephus calls the force behind Moses "Divine Providence"; he reports almost no conversations between Moses and God. The Bible quotes God directly, and Moses speaks to God "face to face, as a man might speak to his friend" (Exod. 33:10). Then God inhabits the sacred mountain (Sinai), and Moses can no longer see his face, and, out of thunder and lightning and cloud and fire, he speaks. When Moses descends from the holy mountain, his face shines, and forever afterward he hides it behind a veil. Here is what Jonathan Kirsch has to say about the influence of this moment:

> The Bible does not offer a straightforward explanation of what happened to the face of Moses that made it so fearful. The earliest translation of the Hebrew Bible into Latin renders the obscure text in a manner that suggests Moses sprouted horns. Thus instructed by the Latin Bible, Michelangelo famously rendered Moses as an otherwise heroic figure with a set of slightly diabolical horns on top of his head! A more accurate translation of the original Hebrew suggests that Moses had suffered something we might describe as a divine radiation burn—his face literally glowed with celestial radiance.[3]

In the Bible, then, God sometimes resembles another man and sometimes has tremendous but inexplicable force. In Josephus, God is a humanlike figure whose function is to reflect well on Moses. Most of the direct quotations from God are rendered indirectly, and what is in Exodus a sign of God's power often becomes Moses'. In the biblical text, we are supposed to hear God's voice; in Josephus, the text only tells us what it means. In the Bible, God has a mysterious name; in Josephus, it is unlawful to disclose it: "Whereupon God declared to him his holy name, which had never been discovered to men before; concerning which it is not lawful for me to say any more" (*Antiquities*, bk. 2, chap. 12, par. 4, p. 71). The note here appended by William Whiston is interesting:

> This superstitious fear of discovering the name with four letters, which of late we have been used falsely to pronounce Jehovah, but seems to have been originally pronounced Jahoh, or Jao, is never, I think, heard of, till this passage of Josephus; and this superstition, in not pronouncing that name has continued among the rabbinical Jews of this day. . . . Josephus also durst not set down the very words of the ten commandments . . . , which superstitious silence, I think, has yet not been continued even by the rabbis. It is however no doubt but both these cautious concealments were taught Josephus by the Pharisees; a body of men at once very wicked and very superstitious. (p. 71 n.)

It is clear that for this translator, and perhaps for the kind of Christianity he professed, the other of "religion" was not "idolatry" but "superstition." But the Pharisees, says the *Encyclopedia Britannica*, "despite the unflattering portrayal of them in the New Testament, were for the most part intensely religious Jews and adhered to a strict though nonliteral observance of the Torah" (p. 623). The rabbis might not go as far as Josephus in concealing the divine. It is not just in religion that it is unlawful to expose certain things to others, but this "taboo on the proper name"[4] seems to be a common feature of the anthropological study of certain tribes as well. Something that resists linguistic form is less vulnerable to appropriation. God does not command; Josephus summarizes the commandments.

No Ten Commandments, no broken tablets, no Golden Calf—although Josephus's text seems wordier than the Bible, it has far fewer incidents. God is not less powerful in Josephus, but we never see him acting. No pillar of fire; no pillar of cloud (although later a cloud over the Tabernacle reveals the presence of God); no telling Moses what to do. God does always save the day at the last moment but utterly unpredictably. When Moses' people are trapped between the mountains and the sea, Moses prays for divine deliverance and says, "and the sea also, if thou commandest it, will become dry land. Nay, we might escape by a flight through the air" (bk. 2, chap. 16, par. 1, p. 76). People are often depicted in prayer, but the link between anything prayed and any outcome is never direct. In Josephus, prayer indicates what kind of person you are, not what God will do.

As we have already seen, Josephus does not seem as concerned with narrative incident as with the cogitations of inner life. If he sees Moses as a rival author, his concern with authorship seems more Roman than Hebrew, and altogether modern. When Moses' father-in-law tells him how his legal administration should be organized, Josephus says, "Nor did he conceal the invention of this method, nor pretend to it himself, but informed the multitude who it was that invented it; nay, he has named Raguel in the books he wrote, as the person who invented this ordering of the people, as thinking it right to give a true testimony to worthy persons, although he might have gotten reputation by ascribing to himself the inventions of other men; whence we may learn the virtuous disposition of Moses" (bk. 3, chap. 4, par. 2, p. 83). Considerations of fame through the writing of books were certainly not a feature of the Books of Moses.

But the lack of concern for story also means that Josephus, unlike most rewriters, devotes just as much space as the Bible to the details of the Tabernacle, the sacrifices, and the priests' garments. Every socket, knop, shittim wood beam, loop, and curtain is in its place. The difference is that whereas the Bible gives God's instructions for building the Tabernacle, Josephus describes the Tabernacle Moses has built. Whereas the Bible gives direction for something new and strange, Josephus describes what priests wear and do with a great deal of familiarity. Josephus, after all, was from a priestly family.

It is from the question of how the high priest was chosen that Josephus explains the roots of Korah's rebellion against Moses (Num. 16). Envious of Moses and Aaron, to whom he is hardly inferior in family and wealth, he accuses Moses of being as tyrannous as Pharaoh and choosing Aaron for nepotistic reasons. The proper procedures were not followed in Aaron's appointment, and Korah is hoping that if they now are, that honor will be transferred to him. Moses replies that he was merely obeying God's orders and that Aaron was chosen neither by personal relation nor by merit but by divine commandment. And the earth opens and consumes the rebels.

After consulting God through the oracle (a more Greek than Hebrew thing to do), Josephus reports that Moses went back through the wilderness, the king of Idumea having refused the Israelites passage through his lands, and Miriam and Aaron both die (the Bible reports only the death of Aaron). Knowing that the Hebrews are itching to fight, Moses demands God's permission to enter into hostilities as soon as King Sihon of the Amorites refuses them the right to pass through *his* territory. God gives it, and they do, conquering the Amorites and taking their land. They also defeat King Og. They win, says Josephus, with slings and bows and light armor, thus showing Josephus's knowledge of and interest in things military.

There seems to be some conflation of Moab and Midian in both texts, and although the Bible and Josephus contain the same elements, their emphases are very different. King Balak of the Moabites and Balaam the prophet are present in both texts, but they play different roles. When King Balak calls Balaam to curse the Hebrews and he rather blesses them, the Bible emphasizes God's will and the Divine Plan; Josephus has Balaam suggest the seduction strategy that tempts the Hebrews into sin. The Hebrews will have the ultimate victory, says Balaam, but you can do some vexing in the meantime. Accordingly, and following Balaam's orders, the Midianites send their daughters to tease the Hebrews, who, succumbing, go so far as to worship the Midianite gods. Thus the idolatry that Josephus doesn't depict in the Golden Calf episode occurs here. Not a word is mentioned in either text about Moses having a Midianite wife. And the Bible says simply, "And Israel abode in Shittim, and the people began to commit whoredom with the daughters of Moab" (Num. 25:1).

CHAPTER FOUR

Frances E. W. Harper

Antislavery activist and early black woman writer—one would expect the story of the liberation of Egypt's slaves to be tailor-made for Frances E. W. Harper. Therefore, it is all the more surprising to see her take for granted the story of liberation from slavery to zero in on Moses' complicated relations with his two mothers and to see all his decisions as entailing a difficult parting. The story sketched out in Harper's fragmentary version is psychological. It is not only about the resolve to leave the high-status mother; it is also about the psychological costs of telling her so, and telling her that he is leaving her for slaves. But Frances Harper's partial free-verse rewriting of the Bible begins there: with a scene called "The Parting" in which Moses takes his leave from Pharaoh's daughter.

Harper's text often follows the Bible, even verbally, but she, not the Bible, seems unduly preoccupied with lips. The princess recalls her discovery of little Moses floating on the Nile (all italics mine):

He wakened with a smile, and reached out his hand
To meet the welcome of his mother's kiss,
When strange faces met his gaze, and he drew back
With a grieved, wondering look, while disappointment
Shook the quivering *lip* that missed the mother's
Wonted kiss, and the babe lifted his voice and wept.[1]

She then recalls her father's reaction to the child:

> And one morning, while I sat toying with
> His curls and listening to the prattle of his
> Untrained *lips,* my father, proud and stately
> Saw me bending o'er the child . . .

The father smiles as long as he believes that his daughter has been impreg-
nated by one of his courtiers but vows to kill the child when his daughter
says that her son is one of the Hebrew children. His daughter defends her
son and says:

> . . . he has
> Eaten bread within thy palace walls, and thy
> Salt lies upon his fresh young *lips* . . .

Pharaoh, thinking of his daughter's mother, spares the child, but as the
daughter recalls her son's vow to leave the palace, she says:

> . . . And thus I saved
> Thee twice—once from the angry sword and once
> From the devouring flood. Moses, thou art
> Doubly mine; as such I claimed thee then, as such
> I claim thee now: I've nursed no other child
> Upon my knee, and pressed upon no other
> *Lips* the sweetest kisses of my love, and now,
> With rash and careless hand, thou dost thrust aside that love.

And it is in this scene of parting from the mother that Harper's text brings
up the contrast between Moses' slowness of speech and someone else's
eloquence:

> . . . for Moses
> He was slow of speech, but she was eloquent
> With words of tenderness and love, and had breathed
> Her full heart into her *lips.* . . .

But Moses opposes her with a strong will:

> ... there was
> Firmness in the young man's choice, and he beat back
> The opposition of her *lips* with the calm
> Grandeur of his will, and again essayed to speak.

His determination to share the lot of his brethren comes from his other mother:

> Gracious lady, thou remembrest well
> The Hebrew nurse to whom thou gavest thy foundling.
> That woman was my mother; from her *lips* I
> Learned the grand traditions of our race ... (Pp. 141–43)

"And thus they parted ... ," says the text, emphasizing once more the importance of this scene of leavetaking. As if it had not been emphasized enough, the next chapter describes the scenes of splendor Moses is leaving. Refusing to be "engrafted" into Pharaoh' royal line, he goes to Goshen and seeks out the hut of his parents, where he says to his mother:

> ... Again I sat
> Beside thee, my *lips* apart with childish
> Wonder ... and my young soul gathering
> Inspiration from thy words. (Chap. 2, p. 148)

"Lips" turn out not to be just some idiosyncratic image but to touch upon many aspects of the story: kissing, eating, speaking, and nursing—all conveyed by lips, and the expression "parted lips" rejoins the images of parting. What in Exodus is parted? The sea. And indeed, in the middle of that episode, we find an astonishing image of lips:

> ... And Moses smote
> The restless sea; the waves stood up in heaps,
> Then lay as calm and still as *lips* that just
> Had tasted death. ... (Chap. 4, p. 159)

The sea is likened to motionless parted lips; the image of parting encompasses death. On the one hand, Harper pictures the tragedy of attempts to kiss a corpse (the death of Egypt's firstborn—"Then burning kisses on the cold *lips* / Of the dead" [chap. 5, p. 158]). On the other, she "Christianizes" the story (". . . how God's anointed ones / Must walk with bleeding feet the paths that turn / To lines of living light; how hands that bring / Salvation in their palms are pierced with cruel / Nails, and *lips* that quiver first with some great truth / Are steeped in bitterness and tears, and brows / Now bright beneath the aureola of God, / Have bent beneath the thorny crowns of earth" [chap. 5, p. 156]) so that death is eternal life. Far from being a tragedy, it is the proof of godliness. Death itself is a promise: a promise of being with God. Frances Harper often wrote poems about dying figures as experiencing a happy parting. Death is an entry into holiness; whatever oppression one suffered in life is lifted in God's kingdom.

Harper also wrote many poems about mothers—slave mothers in particular. She herself married in 1860, became a widow in 1864, and gave birth to her only child, a daughter, sometime between those two dates. Because slavery was abolished at about the same time as Harper had her child, it was not personal experience that made motherhood so large a part of her poetry. But she was always a daughter and spoke fondly of her mother as late as 1895 in her poem, "My Mother's Kiss." The pain of separation is also the focus of the horrors of slavery: mothers were powerless against losing their children on the auction block. There were in fact two major ways that mothers affected, and were affected by, chattel slavery: the division between the birth mother and the owner of a child and the fact that a child "follows the condition of the mother." A slave mother passed to her children the fact that they were "not hers."

There *is* one aspect of leaving the Egyptian palace for a slave hut that has often been seen as autobiographical, though. Frances Watkins was born a free black in Baltimore, Maryland, in 1825. After the Fugitive Slave Law and the Compromise of 1850, no black was safe from slavery, and Maryland was a slave state as the Civil War approached. Well educated and well bred,

Frances Watkins could have enjoyed a life of relative ease but chose instead a demanding life lecturing against slavery, working on the Underground Railroad, doing her best to see that Reconstruction and temperance would succeed. Like Moses, then, she bid farewell to her advantages and cast her lot with the lowly. Like Moses, too, her grave was unknown. She often recited "Bury me in a Free Land"—somewhere other than her birthplace—and her first poem about Moses concerned his burial (1856).

Certainly the chapter she added to the biblical story, where Moses / Frances surveys what is being left behind, points to an autobiographical investment, but one should not be quick to dismiss slavery's role in breaking up the family as well. Frances Watkins lost her mother at the age of three, and much of her novel *Iola Leroy* is about reconstituting the family, dispersed by slavery. She may not have experienced motherhood until later, but she had experienced loss firsthand. And she, more than other rewriters of Moses, knew that choosing something always entailed giving something else up.

In addition, having two mothers and two lineages doesn't conform to the Ten Commandments. God says, "Honor thy father and thy mother," not "thy mothers." Although Harper devotes little time to the scene ("They journeyed on from Zuphrim's sea until / They reached the sacred mount and heard the solemn / Decalogue" [chap. 7, p. 161]), she must have lived by it. Polymatria is something like polytheism: having no other gods before the God of Abraham requires that one have no other mothers before the one whose condition one has chosen to share. One can't have it both ways if one wants to do God's work. And inherited legacies win over adoptive ones: the land was promised to Abraham, and the Bible makes much of Israel's twelve tribes.

Which doesn't make parting less hard. When Moses, in Midian, sees the burning bush and takes his wife and children to Egypt to free his people, Jethro raises no objection, but "there was a tender parting in that home" (chap. 4, p. 152). The sisters and father are separated for the first time.

Why rewrite the Bible in blank verse? On the one hand, to imitate the act of the most influential poet for the slaves: Milton, whose *Paradise Lost* was a prestigious model for rewriting the Bible. There are many echoes of Milton in Harper's poem, and the acrobatics of iambic pentameter must have formed part of her school exercises. Take, for example, the ultra-Miltonic line

> ... day after day
> Dragged its slow length along ... (Chap. 1, p. 140)

Then there is the text of the Bible: that is where, for example, the waters standing in "heaps" comes from. But calling the wall of water "God's masonry," which Harper adds to the biblical tale, brings together the slaves' oppressive tasks and the pharaohs' penchant for architectural display.

But for a person attuned to nineteenth-century developments in poetry, Frances Harper was also affected by Keats ("viewless wings"), Shelley, and especially Wordsworth, who not only helped to popularize the ballad form (which most of Harper's other poems were written in) but also wrote extensive serious poetry in blank verse, including the autobiographical *Prelude*. In an early depiction of a baby held by his mother, he writes:

> who, when his soul
> Claims manifest kindred with an earthly soul,
> Doth gather passion from his Mother's eye! (*Prelude*, bk. 2, lines 241–43)

When Moses listens to his birth mother,

> ... my young soul gathering
> Inspiration from thy words

who can fail to hear the Wordsworthian tone? And in a visibly New Testament context, the line, "my heart leaped up with untold joy" (*Fishers of Men*, line 9)?

Like Emily Dickinson, Harper was suffused with the rhythm and structure of hymns, often beginning with a line—"Onward ... ," "We would see Jesus," "A rock, for ages ... "—that quickly turns away from the hymn that provides its opening. And at the last publication, in 1901, of her Moses piece, Harper, joining a late-nineteenth-century trend, called it *Idylls of the Bible*.

Early in the century, Percy Bysshe Shelley, poet and iconoclast, wrote a poem about hearing about a mutilated statue of an Egyptian king surrounded by desert sands. The king, Ozymandias, thought to be the pharaoh of the Exodus, provides Harper with another arresting image of lips:

> ... whose frown
> And wrinkled *lip,* and sneer of cold command ... [2]

Harper says of Moses' antagonist:

> ... And Pharaoh heard with curving *lip*
> And flushing cheek the message of the Hebrews' God.[3]

Even the Egyptian overseer Moses kills has the tell-tale "sneer of cold command":

> ... His
> Proud *lip* curved in scornful anger ... (Chap. 3, p. 150)

The curved lip, in other words, indicates the haughtiness of absolute power. To which the obsequious lords respond with an idea to make the Hebrews work harder:

> Amorphel was a crafty, treacherous man,
> With oily *lips* well versed in flattery ... (Chap. 5, p. 154)

Lips parted to allow nourishment in or speech out, lips kissing babies or sacred ground, lips curled in defiance, and lips telling traditions from generation to generation—however intertextual Harper's poetry might be, the use of lips to convey all these things is Harper's own.

CHAPTER FIVE

Moses, the Egyptian

We learned what we had always suspected, that the Masonic mysteries were of a Blacker origin than we thought and that this man had in his possession a Black sacred book.

Ishmael Reed, *Mumbo Jumbo*

It was not only Freud who announced to the world that Moses was really an Egyptian; so did the prominent Egyptologist Jan Assmann. Assmann's *Moses the Egyptian* gives solidity to Freud's claim. But it does more: Assmann makes a useful distinction between history and memory, traditions and "what really happened." This distinction suits Egypt in Europe's memory almost better than anything else. It is this distinction that explains the effect of Egypt on Europe and even, by contrast, the image of Greece as Europe's pure childhood—an image of European origins that was fundamental to philosophical and literary theory. The other important point Assmann makes is that the birth of monotheism is the birth of religious intolerance and, in general, that to claim a religion as "true" is to claim all other religions as "false." Thus every religion that claims truth is a counterreligion—defining itself against a specific error. Polytheism always had room for another god, or considered other people's gods as translations of their own. But monotheism was exclusive: "Thou shalt have no other gods before me."

In his search for an Egyptian Moses (having detected his Egyptianness even in the Bible), Freud admitted that the official Egyptian religion was quite contrary to the one Moses founded. Indeed, as we have seen in Walzer's book and as anyone who has looked in a Passover Hagaddah knows, the opposition between Israel and Egypt is fundamental to the Exodus story. Without Moses and Pharaoh opposing each other, there would not *be* an Exodus story. The liberation of the slaves and the threat of missing "the fleshpots of Egypt" have given meaning to many a narrative of freedom. It is perhaps what underlies the idea that freedom means giving something up. Clearly, Moses couldn't just be the kind of Egyptian he opposes.

Freud was convinced he had found the answer to the conundrum in the ruins of Tel el-Amarna, the new capital built by the heretic pharaoh Akhenaten, who reigned for seventeen years during the Eighteenth Dynasty and was reputed to be the first monotheist. First named Amenhotep IV, he changed his name to Akhenaten (Ikhnaton)[1] and erased the names of other gods from monuments in order to worship only Aton, the sun god,[2] whom he represented by a disc with rays ending in hands or ankhs (caresses or the principle of life). Here was a counterreligion, and it was Egyptian. Akhenaten was called "the first individual in human history."[3] When he died, the traces of his ideas were erased, his statues defaced, and his city abandoned. Freud is fascinated by the notion that an Egyptian follower of the heretic pharaoh's ideas had chosen a scruffy, oppressed people to receive the religion he couldn't abandon. Hence the origin of the "chosen people." Freud develops in detail the psychology of this "great man," the original Moses. Freud's initial intention, indeed, was to write a historical novel about "the man Moses," and for that, character psychology was necessary.

As Assmann puts it, "Unlike Moses, Akhenaten, Pharaoh Amenophis IV, was a figure exclusively of history and not of memory. . . . Until his rediscovery in the nineteenth century, there was virtually no memory of Akhenaten. Moses represents the reverse case. No traces have ever been found of his historical existence. He grew and developed only as a figure of memory, absorbing and embodying all traditions that pertained to legislation, liberation, and monotheism."[4] Assmann does a close reading of the "Great Hymn" that remains from Akhenaten's heresy. But worship of "the one" was in the air: in Plato's *Republic,* the three degrees of distance from the real—the painter's bed, the carpenter's bed, and God's bed—make much more sense if there is one God. They often even involve the sun: Plato's sensual sun versus the intelligible sun, for instance. Systems of thought by which we are still influenced today often revolve around a single center.

The opposition between history and memory seems especially useful in the cases of Moses and Egypt. No amount of historical accuracy will counteract the impact of a strong tradition. The mythic memory of Egypt still has a hold on us today, in spite of the facts that contradict it.

Even today, American children's fascination with Egypt takes up approximately the same time in their lives (just prior to latency) as their fascination with dinosaurs. Uncanny representatives of both death and the undead, Egypt and dinosaurs also stand perhaps as the Oedipal parents—Mummy and *Tyrannosaurus rex*—huge and forbidden. What comes alive in them is a vanished world. All exhibits of skeletons, fossils, sarcophagi, pyramids, and colossal statues have a kind of creepiness that doesn't go away. The British Museum, famous for its Egypt exhibit, was offering recently a new possibility for children: "Sleeping with Mummies."

There were two sources of Europe's fascination with Egypt: mummies and hieroglyphics, the realm of the dead and the realm of writing. Hieroglyphics were only deciphered by Champollion as a result of the Napoleonic expedition to Egypt. But the fact that they remained unreadable for all that time did not prevent them from being an object of fantasy for the West. On the contrary. They were thought to embody the things the West considered impossible ideals: they were a pictographic language, pure pictures of things, or they held secret wisdom, known only by initiates. Ezra Pound's fascination with Chinese pictograms had the same basis: they seemed to satisfy the West's desire for a nonconventional, nonarbitrary, writing.

In 1836 an Egyptian obelisk given to the French by the pasha of Egypt was erected in the square, now called Place de la Concorde, where the guillotine had been set up during the Revolution. The unreadable stone, covered with its dead language, was a fitting monument to the act of forgetting that the French were expected to perform.[5] Egypt was also a great military prize for French colonialism, from Napoleon's Egyptian expedition from 1798 to 1801, during which his troops unearthed the Rosetta stone, to the opening of the Suez Canal in 1869. Napoleon's expedition indeed inaugurated modern Egyptology.

The idea that there was hermetic wisdom in Egypt that one needed a secret initiation to know was one of the most tenacious memories of Egypt. When Moses is said to possess "all the wisdom of the Egyptians" in Acts 10, it is this secret wisdom that people have always assumed was meant. And if Freemasons quoted an eighteenth-century French novel for their image of Egypt, perhaps that novel drew its image of Egypt from that same tradition. Indeed, perhaps Freemasonry originated out of mnemohistory and kept an image of Egypt alive that had no basis other than tradition. The fascination with non-Western writing and secret wisdom lives on whether or not any historical basis is found. In the Renaissance, Marsilio Ficino and other writers "discovered" the "hermetic books" supposedly written by Hermes Trismegistus (whose Egyptian name was Thoth) at about the time of Moses and gave new life to the memory of Egypt. No amount of proof that the writings were forged, cobbled together from Egyptian magic books, Jewish mysticism, and Platonism, has diminished the prestige of literary hermeticism. Nor has the fact that the "hermetic books" were first put together by Alexandrian teachers in the last centuries B.C.

In the middle of the eighteenth century, an Englishman, William Warburton, summed up a certain "lore" about and fascination with hieroglyphics before they were deciphered in his *Essay on Hieroglyphics,* the fourth volume of his *Divine Legation of Moses.* He emphasized in particular the illusion of divine revelation in dreams and the school of dream interpretation this fostered. Dreams were considered prophetic: when Joseph interpreted Pharaoh's dreams, he was using a very *Egyptian* method of interpretation. Warburton writes that the Oneirocritics often made the erroneous assumption that both hieroglyphics and dreams were written by gods. Dreams were thus composed of symbolic *elements.* From there to divinely revealed letters of the alphabet is a small step, still in the hands of initiates.

When Sigmund Freud undertook to unravel the secrets of dreams, he began with their mysterious, incomprehensible or absurd, "hieroglyphic" nature. Delving into the unconscious wishes that, according to his theory, a dream expresses in distorted form, he writes, "The dream-thoughts and the dream-content are presented to us like two versions of the same subject-matter in two different languages."[6] Like a Rosetta stone, one might say. It wasn't until Champollion discovered that hieroglyphics were a *language,* not a picture, that the process of translation could begin. In his study of dreams, Freud further refines the notion of *things* in interpretation:

> The dream-content . . . is expressed as if it were in a pictographic script. . . . If we attempted to read these characters according to their pictorial value instead of according to their symbolic relation, we should clearly be led into error. Suppose I have a picture-puzzle, a rebus, in front of me. . . . [O]bviously we can only form a proper judgment of the rebus if we . . . try to replace each separate element by a syllable or word that can be represented by that element in some way or other. . . . A dream is a picture-puzzle of this sort. (P. 312)

In other words, however vivid a dream might be, it is not mimetic but composed of signifiers. These have to be correctly identified in order for the message of the dream to be heard. The *things* are not there for their pictorial value but for their verbal value. The language of dreams represents *speech,* not *things.*

In Plato's *Phaedrus* it is to an *Egyptian* king that the inventor of writing submits his work. Egypt is known as a place of writing. All traditions derived from the Greeks (Plato in particular) see writing as a secondary notation of a primary spoken word. In other words, the Greeks inaugurated the idea of degrees of distance from a primary intention; the Egyptians inaugurated secret writings for their own sake. In the first case, all utterance is a fall away from a primary *meaning;* in the second, it is writing itself that is primary. One of the most uncanny attractions of Egypt is thus the idea that European culture might have a double origin. It might have two mothers, in effect.

Egypt is thus tied to the origins of writing but not to writing's arbitrary nature. A cosmos of animal-headed gods surrounds one, but knowledge is transmitted via secret rituals and kept in the hands of an elite. Polytheism and idolatry rule the world but remain inaccessible to all but the elect. For Moses, then, Egypt is the other, and not just because his first antagonist is Pharaoh. Idolatry is tied to secrecy, and occult powers combine with the unknown. Egypt becomes the home of uncanny magic and hermetic wisdom. Yet the Egyptian system is so prestigious that even the Bible describes Moses as "learned in all the wisdom of the Egyptians" (Acts 7:22). And a Masonic initiation owes a great deal to "Egypt."

Greek gods were like big human beings in the sky, but Egyptian gods tended to have animal parts or to be dismembered and reassembled in a divine way. The anthropomorphism still present in Moses' invisible God (the jealousy, the anger, the interminable voiced instructions) is harder to place in a falcon-headed being who does not speak. Divine but indecipherable writing and silent gods—this is not the usual image of the debauchery of idolatry. Part human, part animal, and secret, the polytheism of the ancient Egyptians seems more otherworldly and concealed than other forms of polytheism. The temptation of idolatry—making a "god" one can worship—the Golden Calf as a return to animal worship—seems to be based on a back formation from hieroglyphics in Egypt, in which nothing is whole. Even what is forbidden is in the hands of the elite. Yet the fantasy of finding the secrets of the universe informs the "Egyptomania" that periodically swept through Europe and America, even though its most widespread forms were in vaudeville shows and other types of popular entertainment. One could never be absolutely sure that Egypt was *not* the real parent of Europe.

Hieroglyphics were often treated as if they were cryptoglyphics—hidden rather than sacred writings. The idea that religious wisdom was revealed and in the hands of initiates perpetuated the traditional memory of Egypt. The history of the West's fascination with Egypt is an important part of this story. As is the Afrocentrist search for ever more Negroid features on Egyptian statues, or the claim that Egypt was an African civilization. St. Clair Drake, in the first (1967) volume of his *Black Folk Here and There*, offered convincing evidence that the ancient Egyptians assigned no hierarchy or meaning to skin color and that the Sphinx, if undamaged, would represent the head of a Negro. Leni Riefenstahl, Hitler's talented mythifier, went on to produce a book called *The Nubians*, a series of beautiful photographs of the paradigmatic black Egyptians in the southern Nile Valley. We have already seen that tradition resurface in the speeches of Martin Delany. Egypt itself presents a racial diversity that can be turned to any writer's purposes. Cheik Anta Diop, in his *Cultural Unity of Black Africa*, argued (and had been arguing for years) that African civilizations (including Egypt) had much in common.[7] He saw them united by matriarchal lineages whose origins were sedentary and agricultural as opposed to marauding invaders, nomadic and patriarchal. His original agricultural society was the one that lived on the banks of the Nile and lived by the rhythms of its flooding: ancient Egypt. African cultures often had strong queens; thus, though historians can claim that Cleopatra was a Ptolemy, the habit of considering her racially nonwhite was strong, so that Shakespeare called her "tawny," Hawthorne spoke of her "full Nubian lips," and Charlotte Brontë called her "that mulatto."[8] It took the 1987 publication of Martin Bernal's *Black Athena* to provoke the ire of classicists who had had enough of this "blackening" of the classical world.[9] The classical scholar Mary Lefkowitz responded with *Not out of Africa* and the collection *Black Athena Revisited*.[10] Bernal in turn produced *Black Athena Writes Back* and many interviews.[11] But as Assmann put it, "Martin Bernal turned, without further warning, from being a historian of memory (at which he is brilliant) in volume 1 of his monumental quest for 'black Athena' into being a historian of 'facts' (at which he is doing less well) in volume 2."[12] In other words, the European ideologies of Greece and Egypt belong to the history of tradition, not of fact. No matter how clear Lefkowitz makes Cleopatra's family tree or Terrasson's novel, they cannot erase the weight of tradition. The subtitle of her book *Not out of Africa* is *How Afrocentrism Became an Excuse to Teach Myth as History*, but in the case of Egypt, myth has always functioned as history.

There is one major difference between Freud and the Afrocentrists, however. Freud was seeking in biblical history an *analogy* with individual development: his approach is *evolutionary;* Cheik Anta Diop's, *alternative*. African cultures are matriarchal; European cultures, patriarchal. When Freud finds in Ernst Sellin the suggestion that there were two men called Moses—the first was murdered; the second, a Midianite—he saw confirmation of his theories of the primal horde, and of latency. The people at first forgot about the murder but then adopted the religion they had repressed. This "return of the repressed" explains many conundrums in the Bible (what is the meaning of Midian, anyway?) and allows for history to imitate individual development. The domination of matriarchy gives way to the original, more fundamental patriarchy. "At one period—it is hard to say when—great mother deities appeared, probably before the male gods, and they were worshipped beside the latter.... Probably the mother deities were developed when the matriarchy was being limited, in order to compensate the dethroned mothers."[13]

Freud sees matriarchy as more primitive than patriarchy, which he says shows "progress in spirituality": "The progress in spirituality consists in deciding against the direct sense perception in favor of the so-called higher intellectual processes—that is to say, in favor of memories, reflection, and deduction. An example of this would be the decision that paternity is more important than maternity, although the former cannot be proved by the senses as the latter can."[14] Freud sees similarities between Akhenaten's monotheism and Moses':

> I venture now to draw the following conclusion: if Moses was an Egyptian and if he transmitted to the Jews his own religion, then it was that of Ikhnaton, the Aton religion....
>
> I thus believe that the idea of an *only* God, as well as the emphasis laid on ethical demands in the name of God and the rejection of all magic ceremonial, was indeed Mosaic doctrine, which at first found no hearing but came into its own after a long space of time and finally prevailed.[15]

Freud's original interest in this topic, it will be recalled, was the enigma of anti-Semitism and the idea of a "chosen people." As he wrote to Arnold Zweig in 1934, "Faced with the new persecutions, one asks oneself again how the Jews have come to be what they are and why they have attracted this undying hatred. I soon discovered the formula: Moses created the Jews. So I gave my work the title: *The Man Moses, a historical novel.*"[16] There are two inversions in this description: anti-Semitism as caused by something in the object rather than the subject and the Jews as "they." Four years later, in his own exodus from Vienna, when Freud fled to England, he must have felt the power of the "we," but then he could publish his *Moses*. He was still invested in Moses the Egyptian. But now Moses, choosing to give the monotheistic idea to a new people after Akhenaten's demise, was more clearly described as a non-Jew, a "foreigner":

> Moses had stooped to the Jews, had made them his people; they were his "chosen people." . . .
>
> It is honour enough for the Jewish people that it has kept alive such a tradition and produced men who lent it their voice, even if the stimulus had first come from outside, from a great stranger.[17]

One of Freud's two fundamental ideas (the other being the analogy with individual latency) in *Moses and Monotheism* is thus the idea of a foreign founder—an idea that many scholars since then, for various reasons, have endorsed. Edward Said, for example, in his *Freud and the Non-European,* writes, "Freud's symbol of those limits was that the founder of Jewish identity was himself a non-European Egyptian. In other words, identity cannot be thought or worked through itself alone; it cannot constitute or even imagine itself without that radical originary break."[18] In other words, what we find in this book is not, as many people have seen, an Oedipal rebellion against Jewishness but a theory of identity.

And yet Moses may be a non-Jew or a non-European, but no one—not even Said—asks what an *Egyptian* is—or was. This brings us back to the question of the significance of the multiculturalism that is fundamental to this story. By countering "identity" with "foreignness," analysis remains on the plane of abstraction. But all cultures are particular. What does Moses' Egyptianness say?

We know that Egypt was the land Moses left. Jewish tradition makes it the land of all oppression and evil. Then what would it mean to see Moses as an Egyptian? One bone of contention would be the status of magic in the culture. Jewish tradition looks unfavorably on magic. It is thought to be a low form of religion. Yet the story of Moses is loaded with it. In Exodus, there is a battle of magics to make that point. In the battle between Moses' magic and Egypt's magicians, Moses wins when his serpent swallows up Egypt's. If you can't do away with something, yours should at least be the strongest. And the sign of magic is "signs." When God sends Moses on his mission from the burning bush, the thing Moses asks to test God's authenticity is a "sign." A magic universe is a universe full of supernatural "signs." All the serpents or red waters are thus derived from magic tricks; and the "signs," signs of God's power. Even the plagues that afflict Egypt are signs of God's magic. The diminishing prestige of magic is based on *human* power, not divine. Or rather, on the difficulty of telling the two apart. When human magicians wielded magic powers, it was a sign of the degeneration of the divine. In order to ensure that divine power would not degenerate, all magic was eventually scorned. But, as we have seen, this was hard to accomplish.

Zora Neale Hurston, on her research trips to the Caribbean, was astonished to find wide evidence of an unofficial black oral tradition of Moses stories. "All over Haiti," she wrote, "it is well established that Damballah is identified as Moses, whose symbol was the serpent. This worship of Moses recalls the hard-to-explain fact that wherever the Negro is found, there are traditional tales of Moses and his supernatural powers that are not in the Bible, nor can they be found in any written life of Moses."[19] Her reference in *Moses, Man of the Mountain,* to the popularity of *The Sixth and Seventh Books of Moses,* however, leads us directly back to the magic tradition. There may indeed be black tales of Moses, but nothing proves their ancient origins.

But to return to the question of monotheism, and to Freud's assumption that Jewish monotheism and Akhenaten's monotheism were originally one and the same. Freud saw monotheism as abstract, and abstraction a further progress in spirituality because at a further remove from the senses: "[Abstraction] signified subordinating sense perception to an abstract idea; it was a triumph of spirituality over the senses; more precisely, an instinctual renunciation accompanied by its psychologically necessary consequences."[20]

But were Moses' monotheism and Akhenaten's really similar? And, more important, were they really abstract?

If we take the First Commandment and the solar disc as paradigms, it is far from clear that the two religions, however monotheistic, were either one of them really abstract. "Thou shalt have no other gods before me" does not say other gods don't exist but that one's own god—like Moses' serpent—wins over all others. Monotheism is structured like imperialism. Indeed, this was the model for dominance in the ancient world; Akhenaten inherited an Egyptian empire he allowed to fall apart. If anything, then, he was anti-imperialistic. But for Freud, imperialism provided the structure of monotheism in any case. He writes, "Through the victorious sword of the great conqueror Thothmes III Egypt had become a great power. Nubia in the south, Palestine, Syria, and a part of Mesopotamia in the north had been added to the Empire. This imperialism was reflected in religion as universality and monotheism."[21]

At first, Moses' God in the Bible speaks to him "face to face, as a man speaks to his friend" (Exod. 33:11), but on Sinai, God withdraws from Moses' sight:

And he said, Thou canst not see my face: for there shall no man see me, and live.

And the Lord said, Behold, there is a place by me, and thou shalt stand upon a rock:

And it shall come to pass, while my glory passeth by, that I will put thee in a clift of the rock, and I will cover thee with my hand as I pass by:

And I will take away mine hand, and thou shalt see my back parts: but my face shall not be seen. (Exod. 33:20–23)

It is at this point, after the Golden Calf episode, when Moses goes to the people with the second tables, that he descends from the mountain with what Kirsch calls a "divine radiation burn" and thenceforth wears a veil on his face.[22] Divinity may be too strong for the senses, but it still has hands. It will take some more turns of the screw before God becomes invisible, abstract.

Akhenaten, too, worshiped one supreme deity—Aton, the sun god. He was represented by a disc with rays—a diagram that seems more abstract than what the rays touch. But those rays, however schematic, end in caressing hands or ankhs—principles of life.

In Moses' Ten Commandments, there is the prohibition of graven images of living creatures. This certainly rules out the Golden Calf but not the most common Egyptian images. Sphinxes and jackal-headed gods are precisely not images found in nature—structured more like hieroglyphic signs than like earthly creatures.

While Akhenaten's Amarna was filled with new images—new depictions of the royal family and even colossal statues of an androgynous, racially indeterminate Pharaoh—Moses was giving the Jews an anti-image religion. It is hard to equate the prohibition of images with Akhenaten's world of images—even when faced with Akhenaten as a sphinx bowing down before a disc.

So, on the one hand, there is a schematic version of the giving of life, and on the other, a god who cannot be pictured but speaks and is jealous. Moses' god may be invisible, but he feels and acts like a patriarch. The anthropomorphism that remains in the Jewish god is in character, not in image. In Akhenaten's Egypt, there are plenty of images, but father figures are bizarre, perhaps androgynous. If African cultures were matriarchal, they might not have agreed with Freud's idea of "progress in spirituality." The ills of which Freud attempted to cure his contemporaries might have grown precisely out of that "progress in spirituality"—the notion that progress inhered in getting farther away from the senses.

In any case, we are left with even more questions than we started with. Is monotheism abstract? What is the real tradition of Egypt? What is an Egyptian?

If Freud's answer to the rise of anti-Semitism was that Moses chose the Jews, then at least we may have a further insight into the troubled relations between Jews and blacks. We may not know yet what an ancient Egyptian is, but we suspect that the "chosen people" were chosen by an African.

CHAPTER SIX

Freud's Moses

The answer is that it is not a matter of gain, but of research.

Freud, *Moses and Monotheism*

Even in the Bible, the presence of leprosy and plagues is an indication, perhaps, of an event in Egyptian history that is never reported directly: the
occurrence of a terrible epidemic. This has led to many stories equating Jews
with disease. Maybe the Amarna episode is figured as a plague, or maybe
the Jews were considered responsible for a plague. Maybe Moses was "King
of the Lepers" and was expelled instead of initiating a liberation, but in
any case, the anti-Semitic tradition, starting with the Egyptian historian
Manetho and continuing through the Holocaust, associated Jews with disease. Because of the custom of circumcision, Jewish masculinity was seen as
damaged masculinity, a threat to the "intact males" around them.

Sander Gilman has studied extensively the biological theories of race in
the late nineteenth and early twentieth centuries and shown how assimilated Jews in Vienna (like Freud) went about ridding themselves of their
Jewishness, so as to "pass" as pure scientists—capable of universality, without
any taint of particular identity.[1] The illness in question had become syphilis
(the bugaboo of the late nineteenth century), an illness sexually transmitted,
to which Jews were particularly immune (because of their endogamy), which

gave the notion of disease a sexual taint and a diseased taint to sexuality. And both became associated with Jews. Sexually transmitted disease passed to the circumcised infant through unclean instruments and barbaric practices. Indeed, Jewish endogamy came to be seen as incestuous, thus entering Freud's domain of infantile sexuality. Jews were thought to be prone to mental instability; they lacked an original "healthy" relation to the soil and had an exaggerated relation to the city (the ghetto) and to modern life in general.[2] If modern neuroses were tied to the "secular advance of repression" (as Freud said about the difference between Sophocles and Shakespeare), the Jews' feelings about the restrictions of Western civilization manifested a discontent that was simply in the vanguard of those of modern man. Freud's method of coping with anti-Semitism was ingenious: (according to Gilman, at least) he gave to the distinction male / female some of the stereotypes he had learned for Jew / non-Jew. Which did not prevent him from becoming a part of Jewish history in his turn. A circumcised penis brought up all the anxieties of castration, and an uncircumcised penis was the norm for masculinity.

Freud was afraid that psychoanalysis was in danger of seeming to be a "Jewish science," which is why he entertained such high hopes for the Aryan Carl Jung. At the height of his enthusiasm for Jung, Freud identified with Moses: "If I am Moses, then you are Joshua and will take possession of the promised land of psychiatry, which I shall only be able to glimpse from afar."[3] Freud and Jung would have had very different responses to Freud's comment, as he and Jung approached the United States, "They don't know that we bring the plague." Non-Jewish adherents of psychoanalysis may have aspired to the place vacated by Jung. Jacques Lacan's bias against American ego psychology was partly against the post-Holocaust Jewish control of Freud's legacy and the Jewish refugees' incorrect (according to him) notion of identity. But some later scholars have *wanted* psychoanalysis to be Jewish, and wondered how Jewish *Freud* was.

Freud's book on Moses is not a narrative but a piecing together of evidence by a scientific researcher. Like most of Freud's other books, *Moses and Monotheism* is a combination of research and speculation. Being able to quote an authority in the field or to point to ruins brings out the storyteller in Freud. Thus he cites the biblical scholar Ernst Sellin to bolster his theory of the murder of Moses and his replacement by another man now called Moses—a Midianite worshiper of the volcano god, Jahweh.

Moses and Monotheism has often been read as a statement of Freud's relations with Judaism. According to that book, Moses was not originally a Jew but an Egyptian, and the custom of ritual circumcision, now often seen as the mark of the Jew, was originally an Egyptian custom. The associations of blood and barbarity that are often the province of the anti-Semite derive, therefore, from that source.

> The motivation that we have surmised for the Exodus as a whole covers
> also the custom of circumcision. We know in what manner human
> beings—both peoples and individuals—react to this ancient custom,
> scarcely any longer understood. Those who do not practice it regard
> it as very odd and find it rather abhorrent; but those who have adopted
> circumcision are proud of the custom. . . . It is credible that Moses, who
> as an Egyptian was himself circumcised, shared this attitude. The Jews
> with whom he left his native country were to be a better substitute for
> the Egyptians he left behind. In no circumstances must they be inferior
> to them. He wished to make of them a "holy nation"—so it is explicitly
> stated in the Biblical text—and as a sign of their dedication he intro-
> duced the custom that made them at least the equals of the Egyptians.[4]

Saint Paul, a Jew who became one of Christianity's first defenders, saw circumcision as a sign of the old law, of literality. The Jew had marked on his body the "letter," which had to be transformed into the "new law" (New Testament) of spirit:

> Behold, thou art called a Jew, and restest in the law, and makest thy boast
> of God. . . .
>   For circumcision verily profiteth, if thou keep the law: but if thou be
> a breaker of the law, thy circumcision is made uncircumcision.
>   Therefore if the uncircumcision keep the righteousness of the law,
> shall not his uncircumcision be counted for circumcision?
>   And shall not circumcision which is by nature, if it fulfill the law,
> judge thee, who by the letter and circumcision dost transgress the law?

For he is not a Jew, which is one outwardly: neither is that circumcision, which is outward in the flesh:

But he is a Jew, which is one inwardly; and circumcision is that of the heart, in the spirit, and not in the letter. . . . .

For all have sinned, and come short of the glory of God;

Being justified freely by his grace through the redemption that is in Christ Jesus:

Whom God hath set forth to be a propitiation through faith in his blood, to declare his righteousness for the remission of sins. . . .

Where is boasting then? It is excluded. By what law? Of works? Nay: but by the law of faith.

Is he the God of the Jews only? Is he not also of the Gentiles? Yes, of the Gentiles also:

Seeing it is one God, which shall justify the circumcision by faith, and uncircumcision through faith.

Do we then make void the law through faith? God forbid: yea, we establish the law. (Rom. 2:25–29; 3:23–31)

Marthe Robert set the tone for many studies of what the Moses book meant for the man Freud in her *D'Oedipe à Moïse*. It became commonplace to see *Moses and Monotheism* as Freud's Oedipal revolt against the religion of his fathers, beginning with the book's opening sentence: "To deny a people the man whom it praises as the greatest of its sons is not a deed to be undertaken lightheartedly—especially by one belonging to that people."[5] But this opening sentence contains *two* statements about Freud's Jewishness: "I deny" and "I belong." This sentence is followed by a statement of Freud's scholarly credo: "No consideration, however, will move me to set aside truth in favor of supposed national interests." This conflict between neutral science (really Aryan ideology, according to Gilman) and Jewish identity led Sander Gilman to devote not one but two books to Freud's conflict between assimilation and Jewishness in the context of the biological theories of race in his day. But Freud's attitude to science was ambivalent: "Science and the majority of educated people smile when one offers them the task of interpreting dreams. Only people still clinging to superstition, who give continuity, thereby, to the convictions of the ancients, will not refrain from interpreting dreams, and the writer of *Traumdeutung* has dared, against the protests of orthodox science, to take sides with the ancients and superstitious."[6]

Two more recent studies of Freud's Jewishness can be categorized by their subtitles: *Freud's Moses: Judaism Terminable and Interminable* and *Freud and Moses: The Long Journey Home.*[7] These books clearly have different concepts of identity (one as a resting place, and the other as an infinite process), but both see in Freud a fundamental Jewish identity, and both reproduce and comment on Freud's father's Hebrew dedication in the Bible he gave Sigmund for his thirty-fifth birthday. The expression "terminable and interminable" had been used by Freud to discuss whether an analysis could be complete. He thought that what could render an analysis interminable had to do with unchangeable human bisexuality: a woman's wish for a penis or a man's feminine attitude toward another man. Perhaps Gilman's idea that Freud transferred racial difference to sexual difference returns here. But the notion of wandering in endless exile versus having a home has long been part of the idea of Jewishness.

Freud's Jewish identity is complicated precisely for containing so much of both negation and belonging. As he puts it in the preface to the Hebrew translation of *Totem and Taboo:*

> No reader of [the Hebrew version of] this book will find it easy to put himself in the emotional position of an author who is ignorant of the language of Holy Writ, who is completely estranged from the religion of his fathers—as well as from every other religion—and who cannot take a share in nationalist ideals, but who has yet never repudiated his people, who feels that he is in his essential nature a Jew, and who has no desire to alter that nature. If the question were put to him: "Since you have abandoned all those common characteristics of your countrymen, what is there left to you that is Jewish?" he would reply: "A very great deal, and probably its very essence."[8]

Totem and Taboo was of course the book to which the Moses book referred for its theory of the murder of the primal father, when a remark by the biblical scholar Ernst Sellin permitted Freud to go on speculating about the Egyptian Moses: the original Moses was killed by his people, writes Freud, and a second Moses (from Midian) took his place, but eventually the murdered man's religious ideas came back. Freud sees an analogy here between individual latency and collective phenomena of memory. He uses a kind of Lamarckian theory of collective identity: the inheritance of acquired characteristics would account for the nature of the Jew.

Jewish identity was therefore indelible—and blank. It had no content but could not be altered. This indelible mark is connected both to the Holocaust and to the preoccupation, in the Moses book, with traces.

> The distortion of a text is not unlike a murder. The difficulty lies not in the execution of the deed but in the doing away with the traces.[9]

> I have not been able to efface the traces of the unusual way in which this book came to be written.[10]

The murder of the father—that fundamental desire in Freud's concept of the Oedipus complex—surfaces here to explain away the inconsistencies in the biblical account of Moses and the stylistic defects in Freud's book about Moses, published in England after his exodus from Austria.[11] Why was it, then, that the death of the father opened up the path to psychoanalysis in the first place?

> This book [*The Interpretation of Dreams*] has a further subjective significance for me personally—a significance which I only grasped after I had completed it. It was, I found, a portion of my own self-analysis, my reaction to my father's death—that is to say, to the most important event, the most poignant loss, of a man's life. Having discovered that this was so, I felt unable to obliterate the traces of the experience.[12]

I will discuss the role of the father later. But why does Freud call Moses a son, not a father, in the opening sentence of *Moses and Monotheism?* There is a way that Freud sees him as a sibling rather than as a father. But there *is* a son-religion very much in question here: Christianity. The son is supposed to be the father's word incarnate. And there really is a murder at the heart of this religion. As Freud puts it in *Moses and Monotheism,* the repressed death of the Egyptian Moses explains the enmity between Christians and Jews:

> The poor Jewish people, who with its usual stiff-necked obduracy continued to deny the murder of their "father," has dearly expiated this

in the course of centuries. Over and over again they heard the reproach: "You killed our God." And this reproach is true, if rightly interpreted. It says, in reference to the history of religion: "You won't *admit* that you murdered God" (the archetype of God, the primeval Father, and his reincarnations). Something should be added—namely: "It is true, we did the same thing, but we *admitted* it, and since then we have been purified." (Pp. 114–15; original emphasis)

The death of Jesus is supposed to redeem the sins of mankind. The "old" testament predicts the coming of the Incarnation. The Gospel of John even begins by repeating Genesis: "In the beginning . . . " Judaism should give way to what has arisen out of it. That is why Christianity is so hard on those who didn't accept it.

But what was that indelible identity, if, as Freud often insisted, it had nothing to do with religion?

As Freud confided to one of his Christian correspondents, "Quite by the way, why did none of the devout create psychoanalysis? Why did one have to wait for a completely godless Jew?"[13] Psychoanalysis, indeed, seemed to be a path away from the normative. As Freud put it in his *Autobiographical Study:*

> When, in 1873, I first joined the University, I experienced some appreciable disappointments. Above all, I found that I was expected to feel myself inferior and an alien because I was a Jew. . . . These first impressions at the University, however, had one consequence which was afterwards to prove important; for at an early age I was made familiar with the fate of being in the Opposition and of being put under the ban of the 'compact majority.' The foundations were thus laid for a certain degree of independence of judgment.[14]

In the flurry of writings that accompanied the "theory revolution" in the second half of the twentieth century, a notable book by Susan Handelman, *The Slayers of Moses,* saw developments in theory as the resurfacing of the rabbinic tradition of interpretation. She outlined two traditions in European culture, which Erich Auerbach described in the first chapter of his monumental *Mimesis: The Representation of Reality in Western Culture* as Hellenic and Hebraic. One of them, she writes, had dominated the philosophical tradition since Aristotle: "Aristotle agrees that the realm of words is not the realm of meaning and truth. . . . For Aristotle, the central act of knowing is a movement *beyond* discourse."[15] The silence of the real and the true is not the same as the unrepresentability of the Divine in the Bible: the difference lies in the theories of language as *imitation* and language as *creation*. For the rabbinic tradition, the text itself is divine, and man's duty is to interpret it. For the Western philosophical tradition, the text is mimetic of something that lies behind it. Rabbinic interpretations surround the text with more and more text; philosophy tries to find the unity behind the multiplicity. The Aristotelians think of truth as a noun; rabbinic interpreters, as a narrative.

Christianity added fuel to the search for unity and the denigration of multiplicity. Neoplatonism centered on the ineffability of the *logos* and the incarnation as the union of flesh with language. The preference for unity over multiplicity pervaded European culture as Christian culture. Between God and his son, there was no difference, and certainly no murder. The son dies, not the father, and his death redeems all who believe. Such a culture also preferred wish fulfillment over nonfulfillment. It tended to want theories "acceptable" or even "desirable." Hence people found Jung's "vitality" more acceptable than Freud's "sexuality." For Freud, resistance was a sign of truth; for Christian culture, it was a sign of error. Freud was brought up to find reality uncomfortable, but the "compact majority" wanted its realities palatable.

In the writings of the major Western philosophers, there is a preoccupation with the Christian notion of God. Descartes wrote about him; so did Kant. Hegel's *Aufhebung* of oppositions gave Christianity a theory that fit it perfectly. In it, life overcame death, spirit, letter. Why would anyone want to go beyond the pleasure principle? Why accept the idea of a death instinct?

In the 1960s and 1970s, many literary theories privileged the generativity of textuality, and thus drew on the rabbinic notion of interpretation. Handelman quotes Roland Barthes as a prime example:

1. The Text, as opposed to the work, is not a defined object, but a methodological field which exists in discourse and is experienced only in an activity, a production.

2. The Text subverts old hierarchical classifications of genres, and is paradoxical.

3. The Text is experienced in relation to the sign, *not* the signified; it infinitely defers the signified. It is radically symbolic, without closure. Its play of signifiers is not a process of deepening, but a serial movement of metonymic dislocations.

4. The Text is irreducibly plural, intertextual.

5. The Text is read without the father's signature.

6. The work is an object of consumption; the Text abolishes the distinction between reading and writing. Reading is playing the Text, and the Text demands the reader's collaboration.

7. The Text is its own social utopia, a sphere of pleasure.[16]

Derrida followed the history of writing and saw *écriture* as a debunking of the *logos;* Lacan emphasized "the agency of the letter in the unconscious." In Lacan's rereading of Freud's specimen dream about Irma's injection, which opened the way for psychoanalysis, he underlined the fact that the dream ends with the inscription of a formula—for trimethylamine—and in his celebrated seminar on Poe's purloined letter, he wrote:

> Our inquiry has led us to the point of recognizing that the repetition automatism *(Wiederholungzwang)* finds its basis in what we have called the *insistence* of the signifying chain. We have elaborated that notion itself as a correlate of the *ex-sistence* (or: eccentric place) in which we must necessarily locate the subject of the unconscious if we are to take Freud's discovery seriously. As is known, it is in the realm of experience inaugurated by psychoanalysis that we may grasp along what imaginary lines the human organism, in the most intimate recesses of its being, manifests its capture in a *symbolic* dimension.
>
> The lesson of this seminar is intended to maintain that these imaginary incidences, far from representing the essence of our experience, reveal only what in it remains inconsistent unless they are related to the signifying chain which binds and orients them. . . .
>
> . . . Which is why we have decided to illustrate for you today the truth which may be drawn from that moment in Freud's thought under study—namely, that it is the symbolic order which is constitutive for the

subject—by demonstrating in a story the decisive orientation which the subject receives from the itinerary of a signifier.

It is that truth, let us note, which makes the very existence of fiction possible.... [A] fictive tale even has the advantage of manifesting symbolic necessity more purely to the extent that we may believe its conception arbitrary.[17]

Lacan's emphasis on the illusory nature of the imaginary order fits well with the Ten Commandments' prohibition of images. Christian culture has never in fact held a dim view of images—there is a vigorous artistic tradition in the Christian West—but Jewish tradition takes that prohibition seriously.

In addition to this new emphasis on the signifier, Handelman cites Roman Jakobson's celebrated distinction between metaphor and metonymy (similarity and contiguity) to say that modern theorists' preference for metonymy over metaphor was very rabbinic: "We might expand Jakobson's distinction to include modes of Biblical interpretation as well, and say that the narrative of the Biblical text is considered, in general, *metonymically* by the Rabbis and *metaphorically* by the Church Fathers."[18] Modern theorists' critique of the metaphorical way of thinking is well illustrated in Paul de Man's "Semiology and Rhetoric": "The deconstructive reading revealed a first paradox: the passage valorizes metaphor as being the 'right' literary figure, but then proceeds to constitute itself by means of the epistemologically incompatible figure of metonymy. The deconstructive critical discourse reveals the presence of this delusion and affirms it as the irreversible mode of its truth."[19] And this deconstructive emphasis on contiguity as opposed to similarity led one person to edit *Displacement: Derrida and After.*[20] Metaphorical thinking underpinned the Christian appropriation of the "old" testament, seen as the typological foreshadowing of the "new." As Handelman puts it:

Through the use of allegory, Paul and the Church Fathers tried to show that behind the crude and offensive letter of Scripture were hidden spiritual and philosophic truths.... And, furthermore, that when read correctly, i.e., spiritually, these same Scriptural prophecies about the Messiah which the Jews claimed had not been literally fulfilled, could be proven to have been spiritually fulfilled; the Jews were wrong in their interpretation of Scriptures because they failed to have the "light of the Spirit" to illumine them to the truth.[21]

The Christian theory of interpretation is exemplified, for Handelman, by Augustine: "The most important figure for medieval aesthetics is without question Augustine.... Augustine's *On Christian Doctrine* was the single most important work on exegesis for the Middle Ages.... Augustine was a Latin Church Father who had to deal with the same problems faced by the Greek Fathers—the educated intellectuals' distaste for the crude quality of Scripture."[22] The aesthetics that dominated that period brought back the dangers that Moses attempted to combat in his flight from Egypt: "The semiological meaning of idolatry as [John] Freccero defines it is the 'reification of the sign in an attempt to create poetic presence.'... Freccero connects this insight about Augustine's sign theory with the poetics of Dante and Petrarch."[23] The allegorical way of reading was at first metaphorical, then later condemned as too metonymical, replaced by "symbol." As Coleridge put it:

> It is among the miseries of the present age that it recognizes no *medium* between literal and metaphorical. Faith is either to be buried in the dead letter, or its name and honors usurped by a counterfeit product of the mechanical understanding, which in the blindness of self-complacency confounds symbols with allegories. Now an allegory is but a translation of abstract notions into a picture-language, which is itself nothing but an abstraction from objects of the senses; the principal being more worthless even than its phantom proxy, both alike insubstantial, and the former shapeless to boot. On the other hand a symbol . . . is characterized by a translucence of the special in the individual, or of the general in the special, or of the universal in the general; above all by the translucence of the eternal through and in the temporal. It always partakes of the reality which it renders intelligible; and while it enunciates the whole, abides itself as a living part in that unity of which it is the representative.[24]

Coleridge presents a good example of the appeal of concentricity, seen as unity, the "one life within us and abroad."[25] Although Muslims criticize

Christianity for worshiping more than one god, this concept of unity enables Christianity to see itself as a monotheism.

Although Lacan did indeed bring something rabbinic to psychoanalysis, and took inspiration from Jakobson for his linguistic reading of Freud, he described unconscious uses of *both* metaphor and metonymy, and was steeped in the writings of the Christian West. In the same essay where he analyzes the "agency of the letter in the unconscious," Lacan gives a formula for the unconscious rhetoric of metaphor and metonymy (similarity and contiguity, or Freud's condensation and displacement). In his various puns on the Name-of-the-Father—*le nom du père* (the father's name; the name of God; patriarchy), *les nons du père* (the father's "no"s; the father's prohibitions; the Ten Commandments), *les non-dupes errent* (non-dupes err; you can't be totally lucid; that is a sickness too)—he places the father in a symbolic dimension rather than a biological one, but he includes rather than excludes the role of delusion. In other words, Lacan's is a *Christian* critique of Christianity: it resembles a rabbinic critique but is not Jewish; it critiques Christianity for fostering delusion but also places a Hegelian structure at the center of it. In his essay "The Signification of the Phallus," Lacan debunks the illusory goal of impossible wholeness but analyzes it as follows: "All these propositions merely conceal the fact that it [the phallus] can play its role only when veiled, that is to say, as itself a sign of the latency with which any signifiable is struck, when it is raised *(aufgehoben)* to the function of signifier."[26] Lacan takes the Hegelian structure of *Aufhebung* (cancellation-retention) and applies it to the transformation into signifying form of human reality, but then goes Hegel one better and sees in this process the story of Christ's crucifixion: "It is Freud's discovery that gives to the signifier / signified opposition the full extent of its implications: namely, that the signifier has an active function in determining certain effects in which the signifiable appears as submitting to its mark, by becoming through that passion the signified" (p. 284). In addition, Lacan is imbued with the writings of Saint Paul, Saint Thomas Aquinas, and the Christian mystics. He calls his ouster from the International Psychoanalytic Association an "excommunication." There is a psychoanalytic place for the monotheistic God—transference—so that man and woman live in a ménage à trois with the deity. Sexual difference does not occupy the central place it does in Freud, but it is what makes the regime of the *One* impossible.

Lacan thus considered himself a true son of Freud whom the Freudians didn't recognize; a Christian but one who found in Christian writings a critique of Christianity (and of the Western culture based on it). Psychoanalysis was for him a reading of the damage Christian culture had done, and the repressions and delusions on which it is based.

As I said above, after years of disparaging Freud's *Moses and Monotheism* and seeing it as Freud's Oedipal revolt against Judaism, there has been new interest in the book in recent years, the most prominent example being Yosef Hayim Yerushalmi's book *Freud's Moses: Judaism Terminable and Interminable.* Yerushalmi is professor of Jewish history at Columbia University, and he titles one of the chapters of that book "Freud, Jewish Historian." The "crudeness" of the Bible compared to Homer, against which classicists railed, was based partly on its reputation as a historical, rather than aesthetic, account. Although there is no historical trace of Moses and, as Jan Assmann put it, Moses is a figure of memory rather than a figure of history, Moses is actually remembered as a historian, documenting what happened when the world began. Indeed, the dominance of history as a paradigm for the "real" foregrounded Freud's "real" relation to his father, Jakob, helped by Yerushalmi's discovery and translation of Jakob's Hebrew dedication to his son Sigmund in a Bible he had had re-bound and gave to his son on the latter's thirty-fifth birthday.

This interest in history led many people to take another look at Freud's writing in *Moses and Monotheism* and prompted Michel de Certeau to include a chapter on Freud in his *Writing of History*.[27] De Certeau shows how the history *of* the text fascinates more than the history *in* the text (Freud's exodus from Austria to England, his inability to erase the traces of this flight from the text, his dashed hope that psychoanalysis would be protected by the Catholic Church). Freud very much believed in historical scholarship, citing biblical scholars to back him up. In the same way, he called his accounts of his patients "Case Histories." In some way, a case could not be completed if it didn't have its past correct. But that isn't what de Certeau takes about history from *Moses and Monotheism.* Rather, he sees it as psychoanalysis, not history, and what psychoanalysis sees about history is its division: to the extent that history is writing, it is subject to all the accidents of writing, and it inheres in diaspora (dissemination), not in a homeland.

> That "element of grandeur" (*etwas grossartiges, GW* 16:236; *SE* 23:128) which is attached to religion is related to "a small fragment of truth" (*ein Stückchen Wahrheit, GW* 16:239; *SE* 23:130) in a problematic of "memory" *(Errinerung)* which is indeed distorted *(enstellte)* yet justified (*berechtige, GW* 16:238; *SE* 23:130), or "displaced" but nevertheless "in its rightful place." Such is the relation of fiction to history. *Fiction* because man has neither taste *(Witterung)* nor inclination *(Geneigtheit)* to receive truth. Truth is what man silences through the very practice of language. Communication is always the metaphor of what it hides. Yet *truth* because, having the right to occupy this very place, something infantile (*in-fantil, GW* 16:236; "familiar to all children," *SE* 23:132) "remains" there: the *"in-fans"* document, the excluded figure, the originator of communicated language (tradition), "the kernel of historical truth" (*Kern von historischer Wahrheit, GW* 16:112; *SE* 23:16), a written and illegible mark, an imprint. In Freud's work it appears as a circumcision *(Zeugnis),* an inscription which is verbally transcribed in the paradox of the "Egyptian Moses," or of the *Aufdruck,* the "impression" of uncanniness, the *Gefühl* (the tactile feeling of what is affected) bound to the *Zweifel,* the "imprint" of the division. Written breaks, mute impressions: an engraved law which can only remain silent.[28]

The historian of Judaism, Yerushalmi, produces a whole archive of evidence that Freud was more versed in things Jewish than he claimed but ends each proof with a pirouette rather than a clincher, as in the following instance: "Is it not ... plausible to assume that one writes important dedications in languages that the recipient is expected to understand, in this case [the Hebrew dedication in the Philippson Bible, which Jakob gave Sigmund on his thirty-fifth birthday] even if it involved a little help along the way? But I shall not pursue this."[29] Yerushalmi is in fact preoccupied with another question: whether psychoanalysis is a Jewish science. This is not a historian's question (a historian can find answers to it, but what is it really?). Which is why Yerushalmi titles his last chapter "Monologue with Freud," in which he addresses Freud directly, in order to ask him whether *he* considered it so. This chapter is quite a feat of writing, especially for a historian. A "monologue with Freud" is like a Freudian analysis. Addressing everything to the analyst, who doesn't respond, is a psychoanalytic, not a historical, structure.

Why does Yerushalmi go to such lengths to ask the question? With all Freud's statements expressing the concern that psychoanalysis would be considered Jewish, and even all the times that Anna Freud spoke for her father, why does he choose what Anna said on the occasion of the 1977 creation of the Sigmund Freud Professorship at the Hebrew University in Jerusalem to ask whether Anna was speaking in her father's name? Why does this address to the dead Freud involve his daughter as his prosthesis? Here is how he ends his monologue:

> Professor Freud, at this point I find it futile to ask whether, genetically or structurally, psychoanalysis is really a Jewish science; that we shall know, if it is at all knowable, only when much future work has been done. Much will depend, of course, on how the very terms *Jewish* and *science* are to be defined. Right now, leaving the semantic and epistemological questions aside, I only want to know whether *you* ultimately came to believe it to be so.
>
> In fact, I will limit myself even further and be content if you answer only one question: When your daughter conveyed those words to the congress in Jerusalem, *was she speaking in your name?*
>
> Please tell me, Professor. I promise I won't reveal your answer to anyone.[30]

Yerushalmi twice calls Freud *Professor,* and the occasion was the creation of the Freud *Professorship.* But Freud's own relation to that title and to the university was very fraught—made worse by National Socialism. This desire to hear the analyst speaking *only* to the analysand is complicated by the same anti-Semitism that led Freud to write on Moses—and to leave Austria for England. Yerushalmi leaves us with the enigma of the relation between analysis and history—and Jewishness and history.

This seemed an opportune time to read the *actes* of a colloquium whose title had intrigued me ever since it occurred in 1980: *La psychanalyse est-elle une histoire juive?*[31] In addition to posing the eternal question about psychoanalysis and Jewish history, this title has another meaning: it could mean *Is Psychoanalysis Part of Jewish History?* Or it could mean *Is Psychoanalysis a Jewish Joke?*

There could be many reasons to dismiss the idea of equating a science with a joke. But Freud wrote about jokes as soon as he was finished with dreams, and, despite his dismissal of the "low" origins of Jewish jokes, and despite their imbrication in a context of anti-Semitism, he used a lot of them. Here is what he says about them in his joke book: "Let us choose one of the 'bath jokes' dealing with the Galician Jews' aversion to bathing. For we do not require any patent of nobility of our examples, we do not ask where they come from, but only whether they do their job, whether they are able to make us laugh and whether they deserve our theoretical interest. But Jewish jokes are the very ones that answer these requirements best."[32] Scholars often refer to Freud's "collection" of jokes, as in the introduction to a recent translation of the joke book: "But he makes a point of extending the canon vastly by adding . . . from miscellaneous sources: from the current comic papers *Simplizissimus* and *Fliegende Blätter*, from contemporary wits (Herr N., Karl Kraus); he slips in little jokes of his own; above all he augments from his own collection of Jewish jokes" (p. xxxvii). Freud is well known as a collector of antiquities; this collection of Jewish jokes was equally passionate but perhaps less avowed.

What, then, is a Jewish joke, and what does it have to do with psychoanalysis? The 1980 colloquium occurred at Montpellier right after Lacan dissolved his school and before he died. Echoes of these events pervade the volume, and it returns again and again to the question of institutionalizing psychoanalysis. What is the relation between the Name-of-the-Father and the institution? We have seen Yerushalmi ask Freud whether his daughter was speaking in his name. What is this but another version of the question of the father's name? The question of the relation between the father of psychoanalysis and the science it has become?

The question of Jewish identity (Freud's, psychoanalysis's) is answered in many ways in the colloquium, most prominently by two non-Jews: Philippe Lacoue-Labarthe and Jean-Luc Nancy in their essay "Le peuple juif ne rêve pas." These two scholars, disciples of Derrida, had earlier written an attack on Lacan titled *Le Titre de la lettre,* in which they demolished his claims to follow the "letter," particularly Poe's *Purloined Letter.* Here, they take any identity as collective, and take seriously Freud's book on Moses. What makes for Jewish identity is the repression of a primal murder, and thus identification and murder have the same structure for a collective identity.

The bulk of the book is taken up by prominent Jewish thinkers—including Emmanuel Levinas and Daniel Sibony—secure in their Jewish identity. During that period also many lesser-known Jewish interpretive texts came into prominence.[33]

One book by a historian seemingly sure of his Jewishness is the book by Yerushalmi cited earlier. On the one hand, he quotes and translates Freud's father's Hebrew dedication to his son, citing Freud's circumcision and mentioning the "new skin" he has put on the Philippson Bible he gives Freud, thus adding to the Freud archive. On the other hand, he still seems to want to know from Freud whether psychoanalysis is a Jewish science—or whether Freud thought so. And he begins his scholarly treatise with a Jewish joke— one, in fact, about Moses. The book begins:

> In a conversation that must have taken place around 1908 Freud told Theodor Reik the following joke:

> The boy Itzig is asked in grammar school, "Who was Moses?" and answers, "Moses was the son of an Egyptian princess." "That's not true," says the teacher. "Moses was the son of a Hebrew mother. The Egyptian princess found the baby in a casket." But Itzig answers: "Says she!"[34]

There are many things to note about this joke. One is the image of Freud telling a joke to a fellow Jew concerning orthodox elementary education. Another is the kernel of his book on Moses. And a third is that this joke, like those in his book on jokes, focuses on the riddle of female sexuality, thus confirming Gilman's theory that Freud replaced racial difference with sexual difference. It is in fact surprising that people don't question the far-fetched story of finding the baby on the Nile and adopting him; readers are blinded by their belief in Moses' Hebrew mother, and the "truth" of Moses' Hebrew birth is a cornerstone of orthodoxy. This is why Freud spends so much energy on "the birth of the hero" and why it is so unorthodox—yet so compelling—to doubt what the Egyptian princess says. The reason this doubt is in the form of a joke is that suspecting female sexuality as untrustworthy, especially when an entire religion is at stake, can't be proposed seriously. The revolutionary nature of female sexuality, which Freud discovered but then sought to minimize, was to be laughed off. The "compact majority," after all, did not want to be unsettled, and Freud reinforced the authority of men, perhaps partly because he could not do anything about that of Jews.

It is this book by a representative historian that Jacques Derrida targets in his treatise on what is unthought in a historian's discourse: *Archive Fever: A Freudian Impression.*[35] The word *impression* is meant to have both the *impress* of writing and the connotation of the Freudian *repression.* In this book, Derrida goes back to the *arche* and to Freud's comparison, in the *Mystic Writing Pad,*[36] of the mental apparatus to a writing machine. The French title of the book, *Mal d'archive,* tropes on the French expression in *mal de mer* (seasickness) and *mal du pays* (homesickness). Although there seems to be no ambiguity in those expressions, the word *mal* does not mean at all the same thing in each: seasickness is caused by the *presence* of a sea, whereas homesickness is caused by the *absence* of a homeland. The English rendition, *Archive Fever,* represents the ambiguity well, except that in French it is hidden—not perceived as ambiguity.

Derrida's question about history, and about the archive, is about how one gets from the inside to the outside, how one transforms the "raw" into the "cooked." History is supposed to be made when the raw materials of experience—collected in the archive—are shaped into a narrative. Derrida shows that the question remains one of passing into representation, no matter how "raw." He takes Yerushalmi's work on the dedication to consider circumcision as an original archive—something written in the flesh itself, marking the body as belonging to the other, an experience that occurs to the subject before there *is* a subject. Derrida continues to reflect on circumcision in his autobiographical text, *Circumfession*,[37] which takes place when his mother no longer knows him but when she is still alive. The family once lived on St. Augustine Street, and Augustine, a fellow North African, wrote his *Confessions*—the first autobiography and an important precursor to Rousseau, on whom Derrida worked a great deal—right after his mother's death. In *Circumfession*, Derrida uses the image of blood-drawing to ask the same question about moving from the inside to the outside—a given of autobiography. Circumcision thus becomes a mark on the body that doesn't belong to the body's "owner." The "body proper," as soon as it has a collective identity, is no longer "proper."

CHAPTER SEVEN

Hurston's Moses

So all across Africa, America, the West Indies, there are tales of
the powers of Moses and great worship of him and his powers.
But it does not flow from the Ten Commandments. It is his rod
of power, the terror he showed before all Israel and to Pharaoh,
and THAT MIGHTY HAND.

Author's Introduction, *Moses, Man of the Mountain*

Zora Neale Hurston wrote one of the few full-length portraits of the man
Moses. His humanity is emphasized by Hurston, as well as by Freud, for
different reasons. Freud strove to present Moses as a character in a historical
novel, whereas Hurston depicts him as a very special person, adept in magic,
able to talk with animals, and learning avidly from an old stableman, Mentu.

This returns us to the question of the role of blacks in Egypt in a new
form—and directly brings up the relation between blacks and Jews. Hurston
is writing in part against Hitler in 1939 and speaks often of "secret police"
and "protest meetings." She is clearly identifying the plights of blacks and
Hebrews, enslaved by an absolute master, both searching for liberation. On
the other hand, blacks have historically embraced Christianity, and, in the
process of becoming "mainstream," adopted the "compact majority's" prejudices—including anti-Semitism. The Holocaust brings to a crisis the limits
of identification, and the Civil Rights movement considered all nonblacks

outsiders. The Jews who once had leadership roles in the movement or in the NAACP were no longer welcome or interested. Jews did not at all consider themselves black, and blacks did not identify with those odd whites. There was a fierce rivalry between the Holocaust and slavery in the United States, over which was most devastating. Yet "black" remained a category of abjection for "mainstream" (white) culture in the United States, where every new wave of immigrants willing to take on lowly tasks was considered "black" (Irish, Eastern European, Mediterranean, etc). And even in Europe, without the constant presence of slavery, turn-of-the-century racial science and eugenics used "black" in the same way. In *The Case of Sigmund Freud,* Sander Gilman makes clear that, "the Jew as a member of a different race was as distant from the Aryan = Christian as was the Hottentot, the 'lowest' rung on the *scala naturae,* the scale of perfection, of eighteenth-century biological science."[1]

Clearly, defining Jews racially helped bring about the Nazis' attempts to exterminate them, and did nothing to increase the identification between blacks and Jews—indeed may have widened their separation. Frantz Fanon could say, "The Jew can be unknown in his Jewishness. . . . He is a white man, and, apart from some rather debatable characteristics, he can sometimes go unnoticed. . . . Granted, the Jews are harassed—what am I thinking of? They are hunted down, exterminated, cremated. But these are little family quarrels."[2] The Jew is defined as "cerebral" by "mainstream" culture; the black is defined as "biological." And both the Jew and the black seem to adopt these definitions. The black person is very conscious of not blending into the "compact majority" and thinks all others can "melt":

> Yes, it would be worthwhile to study clinically, in detail, the steps taken
> by Hitler and Hitlerism and to reveal to the very distinguished, very
> humanistic, very Christian bourgeois of the twentieth century that
> without being aware of it, he has a Hitler inside him, that Hitler *inhabits*
> him, that Hitler is his *demon,* that if he rails against him, he is being
> inconsistent and that, at bottom, what he cannot forgive Hitler for is not
> *crime* in itself, the *crime against man,* it is not *the humiliation of man as such,*
> it is the crime against the white man, the humiliation of the white man,

and the fact that he applied to Europe colonialist procedures which until then had been reserved exclusively for the Arabs of Algeria, the coolies of India, and the blacks of Africa,

writes Aimé Césaire, also from Martinique.[3] What neither Fanon nor Césaire can conceive is the fault line within, the Jew not simply as a white man, but as the otherness of Europe to itself. Césaire is right to say that the Nazis applied colonialist practices to Europe itself but wrong to imply that Jews had not long been scapegoated. White men have only retained their dominance by means of a major repression of the difference within. Yet Césaire presided over Martinique's conversion into a *département d'Outre Mer* of France, while Fanon was a psychiatrist representing France in Algeria. The two men were studying in Paris when they crossed paths after Fanon had studied in high school under Césaire. Césaire became a well-known Communist and Fanon an anti-France Algerian revolutionary, but they both should have identified with the plight of the "assimilated."

Zora Neale Hurston adds another dimension to this non-identification with Jewishness. As an anthropologist, she inserts black folklore into the story of Moses. Whereas Jews (and Christians) see Moses as a stern lawgiver, Hurston emphasizes folkloric and magic elements in the story. Thus Moses becomes a conjure-man and Miryam a two-headed woman. The supernatural and esoteric strains in the Jewish tradition are linked to the blackness of popular culture in Egypt. Hurston does not so much erase Judaism as ignore it whenever it can't be a figure for blacks. She associates the traditional image of Moses with Christianity: "So all across Africa, America, and the West Indies, there are tales of Moses and great worship of him and his powers. But it does not flow from the Ten Commandments. It is his rod of power, the terror he showed before all Israel and to Pharaoh, and THAT MIGHTY HAND."[4] Hurston puts black folklore in place of Western (Christian) culture rather than specifically in identification with Judaism. Indeed, the tale of the book of all knowledge in the river at Koptos guarded by a deathless snake, which is a central desire communicated to Moses by Mentu, is found in a collection of popular tales of ancient Egypt assembled and published by Guy Maspero, where it is called the adventure of Satni-Khamois.[5] His is clearly part of the mania for ancient Egypt that saw it as a place of esoteric knowledge—even if those "popular" tales were created in the eighteenth century. Hurston was affected by Josephus and the same sources as Cecil B. DeMille as well—her Moses gets his story from a wide variety of sources, most of which don't go together. But Hurston's tale circles around Moses' supernatural powers and his central relationships with his male mentors, Mentu and Jethro. Zipporah and other women elicit sexual desire but otherwise seem as possessed by desire for titles and finery as others Moses scorns, following Mentu and Jethro because they aim higher. Moses has a relationship with them that resembles that of the biblical Moses with God—with which no sexual relationship can compete. Indeed, if there is a supernatural dimension to Moses' powers, it is caused seemingly inadvertently by his loyalty to them. Because he learns from and believes in them and they in him, magic happens. He repeats this pattern with Joshua. Indeed, in Hurston's book there are two kinds of people: those who like ruling (Ta-Phar, Aaron, Zipporah) and like the trappings of ruling, and those who can lead (who often give people what they need rather than what they want, and are not liked). Leaders alone have the kind of intergenerational respect that Hurston prefers. Just like the Greeks and Western philosophy, it happens between a father-substitute and a son-substitute.

Apart from this homosociality with its roots in the Bible, Hurston emphasizes Moses' power over nature, and his magic. The basis for this is already in the Bible. There are many pages of description of the ten plagues but very little on the Ten Commandments. It is not God's will but Moses' that Moses die before reaching the Promised Land. And it involves talking with lizards as Mentu had taught him. The folklore tradition blends with what the Western tradition lacks—which somehow becomes African—namely a closeness to nature, talking animals, magic. The tradition of ancient Egypt blends with other outlawed practices to bring blackness into Egyptomania. When Miriam puts down Zipporah for being a dark-complected woman, the reference is to the mysterious "Ethiopian woman Moses had married," but all the traditions of racial prejudice are behind it. It is not even determined whether or not Moses has Hebrew origins. His sister Miriam was supposed to watch over him but fell asleep, saw the Egyptian princess retrieve a "dark oval object" (p. 42) from the river, and only later, to save herself, made up the story of the princess taking Moses out of the water and adopting him. In the palace, on the other hand, the story went that the Egyptian princess, widow of an Assyrian prince, came home with his baby.

Hurston's text is in many ways a response to Hitler—in addition to the mentions of secret police, there is this: "The higher-ups who got Hebrew blood in 'em is always the ones to persecute us" (p. 50). It is the idea of racial purity that Hurston attacks, and the analogies between slaves in Egypt and slaves in America. There is nothing specifically Jewish about the Hebrews. Indeed, the Passover event and the Ten Commandments hardly figure at all, and the murmurings against Moses are ways to ask the question—urgent since Reconstruction—of how a people become free.

In other words, Hurston is claiming less that Egyptians were black than reclaiming Moses for black popular culture. She emphasizes changes in ways of speaking not reflected in her text but related to the whole issue of representations of black dialect. And related to the question of authority in it. Moses becomes the authority who speaks in black English, and folklore takes power over any other tradition.[6]

CHAPTER EIGHT

The German Moses

I.

Friedrich von Schiller, a rival and contemporary of Goethe, is now better known as a playwright, a philosopher, and a Weimar classicist than for his little 1790 text on Moses, "The Mission of Moses." His dilemma with Moses was, however, quite influential in its day. The problem, as he saw it, was to "avoid the double wrong of imputing to the Jews qualities which they never possessed, or of robbing them of a merit that cannot be denied."[1] The problem was that Judaism was the foundation of Christianity but surpassed and subsumed by the latter. Furthermore, the Jews were degraded and abjected by Schiller; how could they have discovered something crucial? He cites what has become the roots of the anti-Semitic tradition: historians other than the Bible, like Manetho, Strabo, and Philo. Because the Jews increased in Egypt in a small space, naturally they lived in unsanitary conditions and fostered disease. This was a way to hold ghetto life against them without discounting their exclusion from Western culture. They carried leprosy, and Pharaoh might have expelled them instead of Moses liberating them. The Hebrews needed a savior.

But how could such a savior arise? Here is where Moses' multiculturalism serves Schiller's purposes perfectly. Born a Hebrew but adopted and educated as an Egyptian, Moses had all the qualities of a leader. He was a member of the priestly class and was initiated into "all the wisdom of the

Egyptians." This was the heyday of Egyptomania—between the eighteenth century and the deciphering of hieroglyphics and the discrediting of Ficino. Moses' belief in one god or Supreme Being was Schiller's god of the philosophes: entirely rational and without figurative trappings. Moses' problem was how to convey the truth of such a god to people more used to idolatrous images. His training as a priest and his initiation had acquainted him with one way: hieroglyphics were instituted to convey the secret wisdom in sensual garb. This tradition of hieroglyphics invented by priests to conceal what they knew from the people who received them was part of the "myth of Egypt" that led to Terrason's *Sethos*. "These ceremonies, accompanied by those mysterious figures and hieroglyphics, and the truths that lay hidden in them, and were preceded by these formalities, were designated in their integrality as the Egyptian mysteries. They were located in the temples of Isis and Serapis, and constituted the prototype of the subsequent mysteries of Eleusis and Samothrace, and of the more recent order of the free-masons" (p. 361). Mozart's use of an initiation ceremony textually derived from an eighteenth-century French novel kept the tradition of secret initiations alive. Later it was doubted whether there was ever any Egyptian wisdom or any secret truth, but the myth was very powerful, and it goes on despite any discrediting.

In any event, it enables Schiller to explain away the people's idolatry or magic, with which the Bible is filled. The Hebrew tribes needed this sensual dress because they were not ready for the truth comprehended by Moses (and Schiller). Thus Schiller is able to blame all idolatry and need for "signs" on the primitive state of the Hebrews and to promote the idea of a Supreme Being as the outcome of Moses' priestly initiation into Egyptian wisdom. Or to have his anti-Semitism and appropriate Moses, too.

II.

In 1934, after struggling with his Moses text, which he first conceived as a historical novel, Freud wrote to Max Eitingon, "I am no good at historical novels; let us leave them to Thomas Mann."[2]

Freud was inspired by Thomas Mann's *Joseph and His Brothers* to breathe new life into the Bible as a historical novel, but Freud's finished product looked little like a novel. The fact was that Freud was too impressed by biblical scholarship to simply tell a story, and his *Moses and Monotheism* ended up having all the drawbacks of scholarship without being convincing. It is a patchwork of scholarship and psychoanalysis—enough to be persuasive to Freud but not to persuade other people. Indeed, many scornful things have been said about it.

Freud would have been surprised to learn that Thomas Mann did in fact write a historical novel—more of a novella—about Moses. Already exiled by Hitler for his opposition, Mann allowed his Moses to appear first in English alongside works by Rebecca West, Franz Werfel, John Erskine, Jules Romains, André Maurois, and others in a series of short novels—titled *The Ten Commandments*—against Hitler's war against the moral code.[3]

One can see immediately that this is a character study. It begins, "His birth was disorderly. Therefore he passionately loved order." It is the *therefore* that sets the psychological tone—and the tone as psychological. Moses wants what he *is not*. This seems to be a commonly accepted truth about human nature. In fact, Mann shows that the giver of the law has transgressed the law: he has broken the commandments he gives. And it is because he is sensual that he promotes the invisible, the pure, the holy.

Mann solves the problem of Moses' lineage and multiculturalism in a way that, surprisingly, was not attempted by anyone else: an Egyptian princess lusts after a Hebrew slave carrying water, they copulate, he is killed, the princess is pregnant. When she gives birth to a son, her attendants set him afloat on the Nile, where they "find" him and the princess adopts him. He is put to nurse with Amram and Jochebed, who has milk from feeding Aaron. When Moses is weaned, the princess takes him and gives him an Egyptian education. Mann seems to have read Freud's version: speculations on "the birth of the hero" (he mentions famous heroes like Sargon and Akki the Water-Carrier) and Moses' Egyptian name. He doesn't mention Akhenaten but does narrate how long it took for Moses' teachings to sink in to the people.

But the most Freudian element may be the image of sculpture—Moses' desire to sculpt his people into a holy nation. This is reminiscent of Pygmalion. In any case, it bodes ill. Later when Moses engraves the tables with the ten sacred words, when he discovers alphabetic writing and writes the first Hebrew, he is described in terms reminiscent of sculpture. Earlier, he had been afraid the people would confuse God's representative with God. He had transmitted from God the laws they should live by. They all involved some sort of restraint; laws against exulting in the enemy's defeat, dietary laws, cleanliness laws. They required abiding by distinctions but not making distinctions between oneself and someone else. In fact, the culminating law sounds quite Christian: "Do unto others as thou desirest that they do unto you." Moses establishes for Israel the "I-thou" relation to God promoted by Martin Buber, whose *Ich und Du* had first appeared in German in 1923.[4] As in the Bible, the relationship between Moses and God is a dialogue. God is not an image but a voice. The contrast Buber draws is between I-It and I-You: the first is the world of experience, in which the other is an object among other objects; the second is the world of relation. Where does that leave the sculptor?

The big unforgivable sin, the making and worshiping of the Golden Calf, indicates that what the people slide back into is an I-It relation, falling back into worshiping an object that has been magically animated to become a god: this is idolatry, celebration, and worship of the gods of Egypt. Sacred speech comes from a mountain: the Bible gives two names, Sinai and Horeb. Add to that the Sermon on the Mount. Mann often toys with biblical mysteries: the Bible calls Zipporah's father Ruel, then Jethro; in Mann, Jethro is her brother. When Aaron and Miriam scold Moses for his Ethiopian wife, it has nothing to do with racial prejudice but is about sensuality. When Moses flees to Midian, he adopts one of their gods—an invisible one they don't care much about—as his own. This is the god who becomes the "god of your fathers" to the Hebrew tribes and lives in a volcano. The god who "chose" the Jews comes from an unimportant god of Midian; he is awe-inspiring as he makes the earth tremble.

At first Moses is filled with the desire to sculpt the people into a holy nation: "Thus was Moses' inclination toward his father's blood; it was the sculptor's inclination, and he identified it with the God's choice and the God's desire for the covenant."[5] Freud did, in fact, write about a sculpture in his essay "The Moses of Michelangelo." Published anonymously in *Imago* in 1914, it concentrated on the *effect* of the work of art on the viewer:

> How often have I mounted the steps of the unlovely Corso Cavour to the lonely place where the deserted church stands, and have essayed to support the angry scorn of the hero's glance! Sometimes I have crept cautiously out of the half-gloom of the interior as though I myself belonged to the mob upon whom his eye is turned—the mob which can hold fast no conviction, which has neither faith nor patience and which rejoices when it has regained its illusory idols.[6]

This is Freud's text about a statue: in this text, as at first in the story about Moses, he takes the part of the sculptor. Although the effect of the statue transforms him into a member of the guilty mob, his search for how such an effect is produced makes him take the part of Michelangelo. Moses, in his sculptor's desire, even sounds like Michelangelo: "he himself was inclined to his father's kin, as the sculptor is inclined toward the shapeless lump from which he hopes to carve a high and fine figure, the work of his hands."[7]

Yerushalmi, finding in *Moses and Monotheism* Freud's fear of having an insufficient historical base and having erected a "bronze statue with feet of clay," sees this as a reference to the earlier essay and Freud and Michelangelo as two revolutionary interpreters of the Bible.[8] Mann, too, seems to refer to that essay, depicting Moses as meditating with his right hand in his beard (like the drawings in Freud's essay) and playing with what began as a mistranslation ("it seemed as if rays emerged from his head, as if horns sprang from his forehead")[9] and then became literalized (the "horns" of Moses, which Michelangelo depicts).

But at the end of Mann's story the statue seems to have disappeared. Aaron's Golden Calf is the danger inherent in sculpture: the idolatry in worshiping a thing, adoring an I-It relation rather than an I-Thou relation. When Moses ascends the sacred mountain to get the tables of the law, he has to learn what writing is before he can write. His sculptor's desire is put to a different use ("he jabbed, chiseled, and hacked at the brittle stone of the tablets").[10] In other words, there are no longer images; only words.

III.

Another German exile in the United States, Arnold Schoenberg, was discovering both his Jewish roots and his twelve-tone music when he left Germany. He began his opera *Moses and Aaron* in 1930 and was still hoping to complete the third act when he died in 1951. The battle between the musical establishment and atonal music and between Christian culture and Jewish culture is fought out between the opera's two main characters. The opera is about what can't be done in opera. Aaron is the only one who sings in a melodic voice; Moses always performs in *Sprechstimme*—a sort of shouting that does not hold a pitch but has only the pitch of the speaking voice.

Apart from Schoenberg's eerie sound, his opera chooses two scenes made for classic opera: the burning bush and the Golden Calf. Aaron makes the calf and represents what the people will follow and understand. Thus the battle is between classic opera and another way. It is no surprise that Schoenberg, having written the libretto for the third act, was unable to write the music. Everything in the first two acts said music was a fall away from the truth. Moses' first words in the opera are, "Einziger, ewiger, allgegenwärtiger, unsichtbarer und unvorstellbarer Gott! [Only one, infinite, thou omnipresent one, unperceived and unrepresentable God!]"[11] As is established in the Bible, Moses, who is slow of speech, speaks through Aaron, who is eloquent. But Schoenberg puts a different spin on this: it is a matter of externalization ("ich kann denken, aber nicht reden [thought is easy; speech is laborious]"). When Moses meets Aaron in the desert, he enlists him as God's spokesman to the people.

The people balk at an invisible god but believe in him when they see marvels—the rod that turns into a serpent, the hand that turns leprous and then is cured. They follow Moses and Aaron out of Egypt when the God promises to lead them to the Promised Land. But when Moses delays to come down from the mountain, the people implore Aaron to fashion them a visible god they can worship. Aaron asks them to give him all their gold, and he makes a calf. The people dance wildly around this image and worship a visible golden god who has freed them. Schoenberg adds an Ephraimite to exclaim that the people are free under lords of their choosing.

Moses comes back and smashes the tables he has brought. Aaron explains that he was continuing the work asked of him: giving the people an image. Moses murmurs:

> Unvorstellbarer Gott! Unaussprechlicher, vieldeutiger Gedanke! Läßt du diese Auslegung zu? Darf Aron, mein Mund, dieses Bild machen? So habe ich mir ein Bild gemacht, falsch, wie ein Bild nur sein kann! So bin ich geschlagen! So war alles Wahnsinn, was ich gedacht habe, und kann und darf nicht gesagt werden! O Wort, du Wort, das mir fehlt!

> [Unrepresentable God! Inexpressible, many-sided idea, will you let it be so explained? Shall Aaron, my mouth, fashion an image too, false, as an image must be. Thus I am defeated! Thus, all was but madness that I believed before, and can and must not be given voice. O word, thou word, that I lack!] [Act 2, scene 5]

Moses keeps lamenting Aaron's betrayal of God, and Aaron keeps explaining that while Moses served the idea, his job was to translate it into images. We are left with the question of whether it is ever possible to communicate ideas without any images, whether all externalization involves passage through the forbidden.

CHAPTER NINE

Moses, the Movie

I.

Cecil B. DeMille produced *two* versions of the Moses story, both called *The Ten Commandments:* a silent film in 1926 and the classic starring Charlton Heston in 1956. These two films are in many ways very different. The earlier film is a morality tale showing the relevance of the commandments to modern life, and the second is a Hollywood blockbuster.

The silent movie is presented with a musical accompaniment: gongs for majesty, faster music for Egyptian chariots and orgies. The silent movie has clear roots in melodrama: indeed, when the medium must resort to written captions to make the story intelligible, it is easier if it is clear what is good and what is evil. The written panels are sometimes biblical quotations and sometimes only made to sound biblical. In any case, the writing echoes the commandments given to Moses: the writing seems like the voice of God. Moses always looks like an old man: neither the burning bush nor the first nine plagues are shown. Pharaoh is always Rameses, when he lords it over the Hebrew slaves and when he confronts Moses. The huge wheel of his royal display vehicle runs over a slave who is fallen. Egypt is colossal buildings, statues, and machines. There is no killing of the overseer, no Midian. Everything is reduced to the death of the Egyptian firstborn, the Exodus, the parting of the Red Sea, the Golden Calf, and the Ten Commandments.

Moses is a kind of *tableau vivant* with his arms raised—either to channel God or to display anger. Pharaoh puts his dead son in the arms of a statue of an Egyptian god and goes after the escaping Hebrews in revenge for the fact that the god cannot restore life to him.

There are two spectacular crowd scenes—the Exodus and the revelry around the Golden Calf—and several divine interventions. Within the multitudes escaping from Egypt, DeMille shows beasts, children, and baby animals: everything is made to present daily life on a human scale. The camera also zooms in on individuals in the crowd: Miriam and Dathan and Aaron. Miriam is at first a suffering water carrier; later the chief reveler around the Golden Calf. God produces the commandments in the air like volcanic explosions; Moses struggles to chisel them in stone. Moses, seeing the calf, breaks the tables, and then we fade to a family scene in which a pious mother is reading the Bible to her two sons—one good, one evil—and in the end the commandments are upheld by their fates. Like Rameses, the bad (and successful) son is a builder; like Rameses, everything he has built crumbles around him.

II.

DeMille's second Moses film is a classic: it has the dubious distinction of being repeated at Easter, like *It's a Wonderful Life* or *Miracle on 34th Street* at Christmas time. It presents itself with much more élan than the silent movie; it comes with all the trappings of a stage play or opera. It begins with a musical "overture," and DeMille himself steps out of curtains to announce the movie's universal theme: man's struggle for freedom under God's law.

Derived from the written captions, a voice-over booms out with thunderous authority the first acts of God's creation story. We recognize Genesis, and all the subsequent voice-over glosses, whether from the Bible or not, have the same authority: somewhere between God and DeMille. All the more because the movie is serious about citing its sources: Philo, Josephus, and of course "The Holy Scriptures," which lead to the quotation from Genesis. The "Holy Scriptures" is meant to be ecumenical: it is not the "Torah" or the "Old Testament" but the word of a vague kind of universal monotheistic God—the same one who appears on U.S. coins in the expression "in God we trust" or in the "under God" added to the pledge of allegiance to the United States, added at about the same time as the date of the movie.

What is different about this movie is the role of female attractiveness in it. Sometimes it involves dancing—displays before Pharaoh or before the sheiks in Jethro's tent. Each main character is provided with a love interest: Nefertiri for Moses, Lilia for Joshua, and so on. In fact, it is in order to save Joshua that Moses kills the lecherous Egyptian master builder, Baka, who wants Lilia for his own purposes. Then Moses learns of his parentage and flees to Midian. Pharaoh's daughter, Bithia, who found and raised him, goes to the tent of Jochebel, who bore him, to urge her to flee. There is a dramatic scene between the two mothers straight out of Frances Harper. Moses, seeking his Jewish mother, bursts in and recognizes Jochebel as the old woman he has previously saved from being crushed by a stone. Moses shows mercy for slaves before he knows he is a Hebrew: he opens the grain stores of the gods to them, knowing that fed slaves work better than starving ones. He is also trying to get ready for the jubilee of Seti, the supposed father of him and his brother, Rameses. The two brothers are rivals for Pharaoh's favor, and for the hand of Nefertiri, which Seti has promised to his successor. When Rameses finds out that Moses was born a Hebrew, he realizes he has won and takes his place as Pharaoh's successor and Nefertiri's husband. Moses, who had conquered Ethiopia and built a city full of Seti's image, is to be razed from all monuments and his name erased. As Akhenaten did to Amon and as was done to him in turn but without Akhenaten's name being mentioned in the movie. Freud is not one of the authorities cited by DeMille.

There is another dramatic confrontation between two women who both love Moses: Nefertiri and Zephora, Rameses' unwilling wife and Moses' Midianite wife—this one a pure fantasy required by the needs of the movie. Joshua shows up in Midian and keeps Moses on track to obey the word of God. Which comes to him out of the burning bush on the holy mountain (described by Zephora). Moses is called.

Instead of appearing in air this time, the Ten Commandments are written in lightning in the stone. But the parting of the sea is similar in both movies: Moses raises his staff over the water, it is agitated, and then a path opens up miraculously for the Israelites to cross: the water makes something like a hedgerow on either side. Moses channels God's power but doesn't see it as *his*. The contest is between man's power (represented by Rameses) and God's power.

III.

In 1998 Dreamworks studio produced a full-length animated version of the Moses story called *Prince of Egypt*. It used animation to achieve effects impossible in live-action movies (i.e., the parting of the Red Sea) but otherwise was much influenced by the second DeMille film (i.e., Rameses looks suspiciously like Yul Brynner, and he and his son have the same "prince's lock" as in the film). The animation allows for unrealistic but impressive scaffolds and vistas. But the drama has a new center of emotional gravity: the relation between the two brothers in the palace. Unlike all other versions, Moses is adopted by Pharaoh's wife, not his sister or his daughter, which means that Moses grows up as Pharaoh's son with an older brother. The brothers are very close but very different: Moses is sensitive to the plight of slaves even before he finds out he is a Hebrew, and Rameses is not. Moses believes in his Hebrew parentage when he recognizes the lullaby his mother sang before setting him adrift on the Nile (there has to be evidence: in the movie it was the piece of Levite cloth in which the baby was wrapped).

In a scene that occurs nowhere else, Zephora is brought captive before the court, and Moses, still a prince of Egypt, helps her escape. When Moses kills the overseer, Rameses pleads with him not to flee, saying that he, Rameses, can make it as though it never happened. But Moses flees anyway, recognizes and marries Zephora, and is called by God from the burning bush to liberate the slaves.

When Moses returns to Egypt, he has to confront Rameses as Pharaoh. He brings plagues on Egypt, but Rameses will not let God's people go. So, reluctantly and sadly, he brings about the death of the Egyptian firstborn.

Suitable revenge for his "father"'s slaughter of the Hebrew firstborn, which was what put Moses on the river in the first place. Moses aches for Rameses bent over the dead body of his son. He is sorry that delivering the Hebrews required it. Rameses waves that he should go, and he leads a joyous exodus out of Egypt. Rameses regrets his decision to let the Hebrews go and pursues them with his chariots. The Hebrews at first fear that they are blocked by the sea, but Moses raises his rod, and the sea allows the Hebrews through, then drowns the Egyptians. Moses bids his brother farewell and then turns to his task as liberator. The film exalts faith, but is vague about it: the song of liberation is "there can be miracles if you believe." *What* you believe is not clear.

Epilogue

My study of the various versions of the story of Moses does not start from the premise, frequent in scholarship about Moses, that he is a sign of Jewishness, or that all these stories are about the *same* Moses.

Even in the biblical version, it is sometimes hard to see Moses' character as consistent. In fact, those enigmatic moments in the biblical story give an opening to entirely different imaginings of Moses. This book, which profits greatly from biblical commentaries, departs from them, too, in not trying to reconcile all inconsistencies and not drawing a lesson from them. The exegetical tradition, in other words, never forgets the question: what does this say about Jewishness?

The central question about Moses is: is he Jewish, or is he universal? In many versions of the Moses story, there is no question but that Moses is the founder of Jewishness. But the origins of Christianity, too, are in the "Old" Testament, transformed into universal "good news." In Christianity, then, Moses' Jewish identity is erased in favor of his identity as lawgiver and emancipator. This universalization of Moses as lawgiver and emancipator is, however, started by Jews, in the celebration of Passover. But the proponents of a judge's right to display the Ten Commandments in his office don't see them as Jewish. Anything universal is assimilated to mainstream—that is, Christian—Western culture. It is therefore not possible for a "minority" culture to universalize.

Two criteria governed my selection of Moses stories: they should attempt a full story, and they should represent many cultures. For although the Bible insists on Moses' two cultures, it still treats Moses as a Jewish leader. How does Moses become mainstream? How does he become what Hurston calls "the Moses of the Christian concept"?

If you are trying to depict Moses as a touchstone for complicated attitudes toward Jewishness from the inside, then Jewishness is a fixed point to which everything else is tied. Fragmentary versions often yield as much information as whole ones (as in the cases of Heine and Kafka in Bluma Goldstein's *Reinscribing Moses*). There are several ancient texts that fill in details about Moses or establish the beginnings of an anti-Semitic tradition. These often still imply that Moses is a known figure being added to or modified. But here the versions of Moses often take him as a cultural hero without reference to Judaism. And when they contain anti-Semitism, it is to come to grips with a shared origin.

By the time we get to the movies, Moses is a hero of mainstream culture, not Jewish culture. How is Moses' Jewishness erased? How do different cultures imagine him? Does an individual author represent a culture? It is to answer those questions that I have written this book.

NOTES

INTRODUCTION

1. John Hope Franklin, *From Slavery to Freedom* (New York: Knopf, 1974).

2. Dante, letter to Con Grande, in *Norton Anthology of Theory and Criticism,* ed. Vincent B. Leitch, William E. Cain, Laurie Finke, Barbara Johnson, John McGowan, and Jeffrey J. Williams (New York: Norton, 2001), p. 251.

3. *The Koran,* trans. N.J. Dawood (New York: Penguin Books, 1997).

4. Martin Buber, *Moses: The Revelation and the Covenant* (New York: Harper Torchbooks, 1958).

5. Michael Walzer, *Exodus and Revolution* (New York: Basic Books, 1985).

6. Walzer, quoting Davies, *Territorial Dimension of Judaism* (Berkeley: University of California Press, 1982), p. 60.

7. Walzer, *Exodus and Revolution,* p. 149.

8. Leon Uris, *Exodus* (Garden City, NY: Doubleday, 1958).

9. Jonathan Kirsch, *Moses: A Life* (New York: Ballantine Books, 1998); Joel Cohen, *Moses: A Memoir* (New York: Paulist Press, 2003).

10. Nahum M. Sarna, *Exploring Exodus* (New York: Schocken Books, 1996).

11. Robert Frost, "The Death of the Hired Man," in *The Poetry of Robert Frost,* ed. Edward Connery Lathem (New York: Henry Holt, 1969), p. 38.

12. Bonnie Honig, *Democracy and the Foreigner* (Princeton: Princeton University Press, 2001), p. 3.

13. Jan Assmann, *Moses the Egyptian* (Cambridge, MA: Harvard University Press, 1997).

14. John Winthrop, *A Model of Christian Charity*, in *Norton Anthology of American Literature*, 7th ed., vol. A, ed. Nina Baym, Wayne Franklin, Philip F. Gura, and Arnold Krupat (New York: Norton, 2007), p. 157.

15. Winthrop, *A Model of Christian Charity*, p. 158.

16. Perry Miller, *The New England Mind: The Seventeenth Century* (Cambridge, MA: Harvard University Press, 1982), p. 432.

17. Thomas Morton, *New English Canaan*, in *Norton Anthology of American Literature*, pp. 139–46.

18. Mary Antin, *The Promised Land* (Boston: Houghton Mifflin, 1912).

19. Quoted in Walzer, *Exodus and Revolution*, p. 52.

20. Quoted in Walzer, *Exodus and Revolution*, p. 128.

21. *Annals of America*, vol. 2, *1755–1783: Resistance and Revolution* (Chicago: Encyclopaedia Britannica, 1976–87), p. 449.

22. Phillis Wheatley, *The Poems of Phillis Wheatley*, ed. Julian Mason Jr. (Chapel Hill: University of North Carolina Press, 1989), p. 204.

23. The use of complex and extensive titles for ranks in Freemasonry resembles that of the Ku Klux Klan, which suggests that Klan members entered the organization after having become habituated to the practice in segregated Freemasonry.

24. Another reminder of the Enlightenment origins of Freemasonry, the Scottish Rite Masons were initially more hospitable to black members than were the British.

25. Robert S. Levine, *Martin Delany, Frederick Douglass, and the Politics of Representative Identity* (Chapel Hill: University of North Carolina Press, 1997), p. 8.

26. Zora Neale Hurston, *Moses, Man of the Mountain* (Urbana: University of Illinois Press, 1984), p. 147.

27. Hurston, *Moses, Man of the Mountain*, p. 93.

CHAPTER 1

1. J. H. Hertz, ed., *Pentateuch and Haftorahs* (London: Soncino Press, 1960), p. 221.

2. Ephraim Oratz, ed., *The Pentateuch, with a translation by Samson Raphael Hirsch and excerpts from the Hirsch commentary*, trans. Gertrude Hirschler (New York: Judaica Press, 1986).

3. Oratz, ed., *The Pentateuch*, pp. 226–27. Numbers preceding paragraphs refer to the paragraphs from Exodus 4 that are being commented on by Hirsch (#24) and summarized by Oratz (#25, #26). Brackets and italics in the original, except as otherwise noted.

4. Hertz, ed., *Pentateuch and Haftorahs*, p. 233.

5. Kirsch, *Moses: A Life*, p. 340.
6. Hertz, ed., *Pentateuch and Haftorahs*, p. 219.
7. Oratz, ed., *The Pentateuch*, p. 225.
8. Or that he didn't speak the language of the Israelites.
9. Sarna, *Exploring Exodus*, p. 61.

CHAPTER 2

1. Hurston, *Moses, Man of the Mountain*, p. xxi.
2. Arthur Jacobson, "The Idolatry of Rules: Writing Law According to Moses, with Reference to Other Jurisprudences," in *Deconstruction and the Possibility of Justice* (New York: Routledge, 1992).
3. Jacobson, "The Idolatry of Rules," p. 125.

CHAPTER 3

1. Flavius Josephus, *The Works of Josephus: Complete and Unabridged,* trans. William Whiston (Peabody, MA: Hendrickson Publishers, 1987).
2. Flavius Josephus, *The Antiquities of the Jews,* in *The Works of Josephus,* pp. 27–542.
3. Kirsch, *Moses: A Life*, p. 5.
4. See Claude Lévi-Strauss, *Tristes Tropiques* (New York: Pocket Books, 1977), p. 312.

CHAPTER 4

1. Frances Ellen Watkins Harper, "Moses: A Story of the Nile," in Frances Smith Foster, ed., *A Brighter Coming Day: A Frances E. W. Harper Reader* (New York: Feminist Press, 1990), chap. 1, p. 141.
2. Percy Bysshe Shelley, "Ozymandias," in *The Complete Poems of Percy Bysshe Shelley, with notes by Mary Shelley* (New York: Modern Library, 1994), p. 589.
3. Harper, "Moses: A Story of the Nile," chap. 4, p. 154.

CHAPTER 5

1. *Ikhnaton* is Freud's spelling; in most of the studies I have consulted the pharaoh's name is written *Akhenaten.*

2. Freud speaks of "this astonishing anticipation of scientific knowledge concerning the effect of sunlight." Sigmund Freud, *Moses and Monotheism*, trans. Katherine Jones (New York: Vintage, 1939), p. 23. And the Museum of Fine Arts in Boston had an exhibition in 1999 of the Amarna episode called *Pharaohs of the Sun: Akhenaten, Nefertiti, Tutankhamen*, which combined the charisma of celebrated figures with a more obscure one under a fictitious name. Nefertiti was not a pharaoh, and Tutankhamen did not worship Aton, but they are the darlings of Egyptian tradition in the West.

3. James Henry Breasted, *A History of the Ancient Egyptians* (New York: Scribner's, 1908), 265; cited in Freud, *Moses and Monotheism*, p. 21 n. 1.

4. Assmann, *Moses the Egyptian*, p. 23.

5. Denis Hollier, ed., *A New History of French Literature* (Cambridge, MA: Harvard University Press, 1989), pp. 672–75.

6. Sigmund Freud, *The Interpretation of Dreams* (New York: Avon, 1965), p. 311.

7. Cheik Anta Diop, *The Cultural Unity of Black Africa: The Domains of Patriarchy and of Matriarchy in Classical Antiquity* (Chicago: Third World Press, 1978).

8. Nathaniel Hawthorne, *The Marble Faun* (New York: Penguin, 1990), p. 126; Charlotte Brontë, *Villette* (New York: Penguin, 1979), p. 282.

9. Martin Bernal, *Black Athena: The Afroasiatic Roots of Classical Civilization* (New Brunswick, NJ: Rutgers University Press, 1987).

10. Mary R. Lefkowitz, *Not Out of Africa: How Afrocentrism Became an Excuse to Teach Myth as History* (New York: Basic Books, 1997); Lefkowitz and Guy MacLean Rogers, eds., *Black Athena Revisited* (Chapel Hill: University of North Carolina Press, 1996).

11. Martin Bernal, *Black Athena Writes Back: Martin Bernal Responds to His Critics*, ed. David Chioni Moore (Durham, NC: Duke University Press, 2001).

12. Assmann, *Moses the Egyptian*, p. 13.

13. Freud, *Moses and Monotheism*, pp. 105–6.

14. Freud, *Moses and Monotheism*, pp. 150–51.

15. Freud, *Moses and Monotheism*, pp. 27, 82.

16. Ernst L. Freud, ed., *The Letters of Sigmund Freud and Arnold Zweig*, trans. William Robson-Scott and Elaine Robson-Scott (New York: New York University Press, 1987), p. 91.

17. Freud, *Moses and Monotheism*, pp. 55, 63.

18. Edward Said, *Freud and the Non-European* (London: Verso, 2004), p. 54.

19. Zora Neale Hurston, *Tell My Horse* (Berkeley, CA: Turtle Island, 1981), p. 139.

20. Freud, *Moses and Monotheism*, p. 144.

21. Freud, *Moses and Monotheism*, p. 22.

22. Kirsch, *Moses: A Life*, p. 5.

CHAPTER 6

1. Sander Gilman, *Freud, Race, and Gender* (Princeton, NJ: Princeton University Press, 1993).

2. See Gilman: "In 1907, Georges Wulfung-Luer published a detailed study of the Jews' predisposition to nervous diseases in which he traced this predisposition back to biblical times, attempting to counter the argument of the situational causation of the nervousness of the Jews. Such views were espoused by noteworthy opponents to political anti-Semitism, such as the French historian Anatole Leroy-Beaulieu. He, too, agreed that 'the Jew is particularly liable to the disease of our age, neurosis.' He wrote that 'the Jew is the most nervous of men, perhaps because he is the most "cerebral," because he has lived most by his brain.' He is 'the most nervous, and, in so far, the most modern of men.'" (*Freud, Race, and Gender*, p. 95).

3. Letter of January 17, 1909, in *The Freud-Jung Letters,* ed. William McGuire, trans. Ralph Manheim and R. F. C. Hull (Princeton, NJ: Princeton University Press, 1974), pp. 196–97.

4. Freud, *Moses and Monotheism,* pp. 33–34.

5. Freud, *Moses and Monotheism,* p. 3.

6. Wilhelm Jensen / Sigmund Freud, *Gradival Delusion and Dream in Wilhelm Jensen's Gradiva* (Los Angeles: Sun and Moon Press, 1992), pp. 121–22.

7. Yosef Hayim Yerushalmi, *Freud's Moses: Judaism Terminable and Interminable* (New Haven: Yale University Press, 1991); Emanuel Rice, *Freud and Moses: The Long Journey Home* (Albany: State University of New York Press, 1990).

8. Sigmund Freud, *Totem and Taboo* (New York: Norton, 1950), p. xxxi.

9. Freud, *Moses and Monotheism,* p. 52.

10. Freud, *Moses and Monotheism,* p. 131.

11. Susan Handelman quotes Freud on disbanding the psychoanalytic movement and leaving Austria after the Anschluss: "After the destruction of the temple in Jerusalem by Titus, Rabbi Jochanan ben Zakkai asked for permission to open a school at Yavneh for the study of the Torah. We are going to do the same. We, after all, are accustomed by our history and tradition, and some of us by our personal experience, to being persecuted" (Susan A. Handelman, *The Slayers of Moses: The Emergence of Rabbinic Interpretation in Modern Literary Theory* [Albany: State University of New York Press, 1982], p. 151). The rebuilding of the second temple, it will be recalled, is one of the aims of Freemasonry. Despite Freemasonry's often obvious Christian affinities, Jews and Freemasons were often subject to the same prejudices in Europe.

12. Sigmund Freud, Preface to the second edition, *The Interpretation of Dreams,* trans. James Strachey (New York: Avon, 1965), p. xxvi.

13. Freud to Oskar Pfister, October 9, 1918; quoted in Peter Gay, *A Godless Jew* (New Haven: Yale University Press, 1987), front matter.

14. Sigmund Freud, *An Autobiographical Study,* trans. James Strachey (New York: Norton, 1952), pp. 14–15.

15. Handelman, *The Slayers of Moses,* p. 7.

16. Handelman, *The Slayers of Moses,* p. 80.

17. Jacques Lacan, "Seminar on 'The Purloined Letter,'" trans. Jeffrey Mehlman, in *The Purloined Poe: Lacan, Derrida, and Psychoanalytic Reading,* ed. John P. Muller and William J. Richardson (Baltimore: Johns Hopkins University Press, 1988), pp. 28–29; original emphasis.

18. Handelman, *The Slayers of Moses,* p. 77.

19. De Man, quoted in David Richter, *The Critical Tradition* (New York: St. Martin's Press, 1989), p. 1021.

20. Mark Krupnick, ed., *Displacement: Derrida and After* (Bloomington: Indiana University Press, 1983).

21. Handelman, *The Slayers of Moses,* p. 86.

22. Handelman, *The Slayers of Moses,* p. 111.

23. Handelman, *The Slayers of Moses,* p. 118, referring to John Freccero, "The Fig Tree and the Laurel: Petrarch's Poetics," *Diacritics* 5 (1975): 38.

24. S. T. Coleridge, *The Portable Coleridge,* ed. I. A. Richards (New York: Viking, 1950), p. 388; original emphasis.

25. Coleridge, "The Eolian Harp," line 26, in *The Portable Coleridge,* p. 66.

26. Jacques Lacan, *Écrits,* trans. Alan Sheridan (New York: Norton, 1977), p. 288.

27. Michel de Certeau, *Writing of History,* trans. Tom Conley (New York: Columbia University Press, 1988).

28. De Certeau, *Writing of History,* p. 345.

29. Yerushalmi, *Freud's Moses,* p. 72.

30. Yerushalmi, *Freud's Moses,* p. 100.

31. *La Psychanalyse est-elle une histoire juive? Colloque de Montpellier, 1980* (Paris: Seuil, 1981).

32. Sigmund Freud, *The Joke and Its Relation to the Unconscious,* trans. Joyce Crick (New York: Penguin, 2002), pp. 38–39.

33. See especially Harold Bloom, *Kabbalah and Criticism* (New York: Continuum, 2005); Sanford Budick and Geoffrey Hartman, eds., *Midrash and Literature* (New Haven: Yale University Press, 1986).

34. Yerushalmi, *Freud's Moses,* p. 1.

35. Jacques Derrida, *Archive Fever: A Freudian Impression,* trans. Eric Prenowitz (Chicago: University of Chicago Press, 1996).

36. See Jacques Derrida, "Freud and the Scene of Writing," in *Writing and Difference,* trans. Alan Bass (Chicago: University of Chicago Press, 1978), pp. 196–231.

37. Jacques Derrida and Geoffrey Bennington, *Circumfession* (Chicago: University of Chicago Press, 1993).

CHAPTER 7

1. Sander Gilman, *The Case of Sigmund Freud* (Baltimore: Johns Hopkins University Press, 1993), p. 12.

2. Frantz Fanon, *Black Skin, White Masks,* trans. Charles Markman (New York: Grove Press, 1967), p. 115.

3. Aimé Césaire, *Discourse on Colonialism,* trans. Joan Pinkham (New York: Monthly Review Press, 1972), p. 14.

4. Hurston, *Moses, Man of the Mountain,* p. xxii.

5. Guy Maspero, *Contes populaires de l'Egypte ancienne* (Paris: Guilmoto, 1906), pp. 100–129.

6. See also Barbara Johnson, "Moses and Intertextuality: Sigmund Freud, Zora Neale Hurston, and the Bible," in Bainard Cowan and Jefferson Humphries, eds., *Poetics of the Americas: Race, Founding, and Textuality* (Baton Rouge: Louisiana State University Press, 1997), pp. 15–29.

CHAPTER 8

1. *Schiller's Complete Works,* ed. and trans. Charles J. Hempel (Philadelphia: I. Kohler, 1861), vol. 2, p. 358.

2. Yerushalmi, *Freud's Moses,* p. 18.

3. Thomas Mann, "The First Commandment," trans. George R. Marek, in *The Ten Commandments* (New York: Simon and Schuster, 1943). Subsequently published in German as *Das Gesetz* in 1944, and in a new translation as *The Tables of the Law,* trans. H. T. Lowe-Porter (New York: A. A. Knopf, 1945).

4. Martin Buber, *I and Thou,* new translation and introduction by Walter Kaufmann (New York: Simon and Schuster, 1970).

5. Mann, "The First Commandment," p. 15.

6. Sigmund Freud, *Character and Culture,* ed. Philippe Rieff (New York: Collier, 1963), pp. 82–83.

7. Mann, "The First Commandment," p. 5.

8. Yerushalmi, *Freud's Moses,* p. 22.

9. Mann, "The First Commandment," p. 59.

10. Mann, "The First Commandment," p. 60.

11. Karl H. Wörner, *Schoenberg's 'Moses and Aaron'* (London: St. Martin's Press, 1963), p. 112.

INDEX

Aaron, 19–20, 21, 23, 37–38, 87

African culture, 11, 14, 51–52

Akhenaten, 47, 56–57, 84, 91, 99n1, 100n2

allegory, 1–2, 34

Amarna episode, 47, 57, 58, 100

Amram, 32, 84

ankh, 47, 56

anthropomorphism, 51, 57

Antin, Mary, 12

Antiquities of the Jews (Josephus), 31–33, 35

anti-Semitism: abjection of Jews and, 82, 83; blood and barbarity associated with, 60; in Europe, 53–54, 57, 59, 101n11; Freud and, 53–54, 57, 59; Nazi Holocaust and, 58; roots of, 82, 96

Archive Fever (Derrida), 75

archives, and history, 75–76

Aristotle, 65

Assmann, Jan, 10, 46, 47, 52, 70

Aton, sun god, 47, 56, 100n2

Auerbach, Erich, 64

Autobiographical Study (Freud), 64

Barthes, Roland, 65–66

Bernal, Martin, 52

the Bible: allegory in, 34; circumcision as metaphor in, 21; defined, 5; God's characteristics in, 35; God's word and, 35; Hebrew, 35; history as analogy and, 52–53; inconsistencies in, 95; Latin, 35; laws in, 20–22; literary style in, 35; mysteries in, 85; as "old testament," 2, 67–68; Philippson, 71, 74. *See also* Books of Moses

biblical Moses: as author of Books of Moses, 22, 37; birth and rescue of, 30–31, 75; circumcision and, 18, 21; Egyptian overseer killed by, 31; God seeking to kill, or confront, 16–18; Golden Calf and, 7, 20–22, 28; as leader of Jews, 96; mother of, 31, 32, 84; polygamy and, 23–24; on shining face or rays emerging from head of Moses, 35, 56; speech impediment of, 19–21; story of, 16; the Tabernacle and, 16, 20–23, 28, 36–37; two cultures of, 96. *See also* the Egyptian Moses

birth and rescue of Moses, 30–34, 75, 80–81, 92

Black Athena Revisited (Lefkowitz), 52

90–91; the Ten Commandments and, 89, 91–92; Zephora (Zipporah) in, 91, 92
Mozart, Wolfgang, 11, 83
multiculturalism, x–xi, 1, 2–3, 54–55, 82, 96
Mumbo Jumbo (Reed), 46
"My Mother's Kiss" (Harper), 42

Nancy, Jean-Luc, 74
nationalism and nation building, 1, 9–10, 15
Nazi Holocaust, 7, 58, 59, 63, 77, 78–79, 81
Nefertiri, 91, 100n2
The *New English Canaan* (Morton), 12
New Testament, 4, 29–30, 34, 36, 60–61, 64. *See also* the Bible; Christianity
Not out of Africa (Lefkowitz), 52
The Nubians (Riefenstahl), 52

Oedipus complex, 48, 54, 61, 63, 70
Old Testament, 2, 67–68. *See also* the Bible
opera, of Moses story, 20, 87–88
oral law, 26
the Other, 4–5, 36, 51, 75–76, 79, 85
overseer, killed by Moses, 15, 31, 91, 92

Palestine, 8
Paradise Lost (Milton), 43–45
"The Parting" (Harper), 39–40
parting of the sea, 34, 41–42, 92, 93
Passover, 1, 3–4, 47, 81, 95
patriarchy, 52–53
Paul (saint), on circumcised spirit, 18, 60–61
Pentateuch (Hertz), 17, 19, 20
Pentateuch (Hirsch), 17–18, 20
"Le peuple juif ne rêve pas" (Lacoue-Labarthe and Nancy), 74
Phaedrus (Plato), 50
Philippson Bible, 71, 74
philosophical tradition, 5, 46, 64–65, 80
plagues, 34, 42, 55, 58, 89–90, 92–93
Plato, 48, 49, 50
polygamy, 23–24
prayer, 4, 32, 37

Prelude (Harper), 44
priesthood, 21, 37, 82
Prince of Egypt (movie), 92–93
Promised Land, 7, 11–12, 16, 28, 59, 80, 87
The Promised Land (Antin), 12
psychoanalysis, 53–54, 59, 64, 70, 71–73, 74, 84
psychology, in Moses story, 31, 34, 37, 84
Puritans, 11–12

rabbinic tradition, 20, 36, 64–66, 67, 69
race: racial difference transferred to sexual difference and, 62, 75; racial purity and, 78, 81
racism, 11, 13, 24
Raguel, 35, 37. *See also* Jethro
Rameses, 89, 90, 91, 92, 93
Reed, Ishmael, 46
religions: counterreligion and, 46, 47; intolerance of, 46; religious freedom in the New World colonies and, 11–14. *See also* monotheism; *specific religions*
Republic (Plato), 48
Reuel, 35. *See also* Jethro
The Revelation and the Covenant (Buber), 5–6
Rice, Emanuel, 62
Riefenstahl, Leni, 52
Robert, Marthe, 61–62
Rosetta stone, 49, 50

Said, Edward, 54
Sarna, Nahum, 8–9, 20
Satni-Khamois, adventure of, 80
Schiller, Friedrich von, 82–83
Schoenberg, Arnold, 87–88
scholarship: on Books of Moses, 5–9; on Moses story, 70–71, 84, 86, 95
scientific research, and Moses story, 59–60, 61
sculpture images, and Moses, 84–87
the Second Commandment, 4–5, 57, 67
Sellin, Ernst, 52–53, 60
"Semiology and Rhetoric" (de Man), 67

Text & display:	Janson
Compositor:	BookMatters, Berkeley
Indexer:	Naomi Linzer
Printer & binder:	Odyssey Press